WHY I WAS

MW01601158

BY DONALD A. DREXLER

Published by Starry Night Publishing.Com
Rochester, New York

Copyright 2024 Donald A. Drexler

Donald A. Drexler

Foreword by Mike Drexler

My dad first proposed to write some of his Xerox work stories into a book during the Corona Virus pandemic which began in 2020. If you are stuck at home with a computer, you might as well write a book!

You should know that my dad was 85 when he came up with the idea to write a book. I told him I would assist him with some typing and minor editing before he turned that over to professionals.

Warning: this book is written by an Engineer. Engineers have their own way of talking, thinking and acting. Lawyers and medical professionals likewise use their own language.

My dad's 30-year career at Xerox Corporation took him through Xerox's heyday. There were many interesting and successful products going out to market. Some were revolutionary for their time. Some were gigantic and extremely complicated. The Webster, NY manufacturing campus was bustling.

I describe my dad's career as a manufacturing trouble-shooter. He would be assigned problems in the manufacturing process and be expected to come up with a solution. He was there at a time when many workers had a sense of mutual company loyalty. He would find solutions that would benefit Xerox Corporation and often protect the company image. Of course, not everyone felt that way. Some of my dad's chapters deal with those conflicts with personnel. I wonder if the company's success did not tempt some individuals with selfish motives and greed. Hence the stories of company theft, sabotage, denial that parts were defective, and sometimes non-cooperation with a small group of union employees as well as the bureaucracy of upper management. You will read how some people seemed to care less about the company than lining their own pockets. Please do not get the idea that my dad being an engineer was against the union. He tried to work with everyone and met many wonderful hard-working people from all walks of life. One of his work goals was to keep the assembly line going. That entailed making sure the part supplies met the quality standards and that the assembly process ran smoothly (if it didn't then trouble-shoot and solve the problem). There are some chapters where you may disagree with my dad's approach or perhaps his communication style. This book is not a "how to" (do it his way) and your problems will be solved. His intent was to inspire all to do the right thing for the company. I hope you will be inspired to do something even better.

PREFACE

Initially I never thought I would write this book. My contemplation grew after being retired for over twenty-five years. My son Michael supported me in putting this book together.

Funds from this book will help support a youth *Anti-Drug and Alcohol Poster Contest* I have been running for twenty years.

It became apparent that I needed to develop this book for future engineers, managers, or anyone, should they be determined to resolve serious problems. You will need willpower, courage, energy, and devotion.

All chapters are of true events with real problems, with one mission in mind, to obtain exceptional results. As you read these chapters you will find italicized words. Whenever a name, event or place is italicized, it is actual or authentic. All personal names except three, have been changed to protect the innocent or the guilty.

In many of these chapters there was no turning back, you might call it turbulent times. My desire here is to inspire or stimulate you to do the right thing. Doing this, the results will always be rewarding. However, at times the problems will turn into nightmares. When this happens, you will have to consider the facts and never second guess. Spending additional time reviewing the problem, you will be astonished by your findings. Never give up and always take advantage of opportunities.

There are good examples of the importance of perseverance. Understand it is worth fighting for, such as keeping the *Xerox* image first, the possibilities can be endless. Perseverance helped me many times down a new path that paid off well.

As you read these chapters you will find I would abandon some principles, be unyielding and relentless. This was only done for the good and wellbeing of the company. What I wanted most at *Xerox Corporation* was to follow in the footsteps of the early pioneers and get the product out the door. I always wanted to make an important contribution to *Xerox Corporation.*

I never believed in people who were motivated in their actions which were entirely selfish, or those whose intent was division. It did happen and I would take them "Head-on". If there was ever an exception to the rule (with *Xerox policies and procedures*) by me, it would be done for the benefit of *Xerox Corporation.*

The key to effectiveness is being good natured, having determination and focusing on your goal to achieve your dreams.

I made sure that I was always communicating with top managers or the *Vice President.*

My main goal was to serve my managers and the people with whom I worked with. There is a common good and a way forward if you can inspire others to do the right thing to obtain the best result.

Valuable lessons are learned in these chapters about challenges and achievements. The true value of an engineer or manager is the importance of being creative and productive.

Donald A. Drexler
Marking Imaging Program
Engineering Reliability Manager (retired)
Xerox Corporation
Webster, New York

INTRODUCTION

This book is about my 30 years working at *Xerox Corporation*. This is a brief history of my employment which covered many position titles such as *Manufacturing Standards Technician, Manufacturing Fabrication Engineer, Photoreceptor Engineer, Photoreceptor Project Manager, Mid Volume Engineer, Advanced Manufacturing Engineer, High Volume Engineer, Senior Engineer, and Marking Imaging Program - Engineering Reliability Manager*. Not many people moved through titles like this.

My early days were a steppingstone into the future with *Xerox Corporation*. I always wanted to inspire and strive for a better company. I wanted to immerse myself along with my natural ability to resolve problems. Some engineers and managers thought I had inherent abilities for resolving problems. I couldn't account for those inherent abilities. If there were engineering boundaries, I would push them to the limit, if there were challenges, I would meet them head on. I was determined to never give up. It was evident at times, the magnitude of problems influenced my resourcefulness, at times I was forced to break the rules. All I wanted to do, was to reach out to others, "to inspire them to do the same and get to the end result."

The people that I worked with were brilliant and some were geniuses from all walks of life. I loved working on high-cost problems, and some were over a million dollars. Sometimes it took incredible ingenuity and perseverance to resolve the problem. Each problem resulted in a very positive resolution. It was a challenge at times, especially when there was no end in sight, and knowing that, it created more energy. If I had to break the rules, it was to influence others' thinking. At the same time, I was committed to protecting the *Xerox Corporate* image.

I recognized there were sensitive personnel situations, and I will be straight forward, and honest with the facts. If there was a *Proprietary Process,* it will not be mentioned.

Within this book there are no photographs of *Xerox copiers, duplicators, and printers.* This was because my lawyer failed in obtaining copyright permission to publish photographs of copiers, duplicators and printers that are no longer manufactured or sold. Some of the chapters that I worked with include only a brief description of their capabilities in the Appendixes. For information about various *Xerox* copiers, duplicators, and printers go to http://xeroxnostalgia.com .

For thirty years — I was Blessed to work with many of the most keen and brilliant employees at *Xerox Corporation.* I learned many management skills from these people that guided me through many managerial projects. I will always be grateful to these people for their assistance.

This book is dedicated to engineers, managers and everyone who has worked for a corporation or a business, that can help or guide them toward a better future.

> ***Donald A. Drexler***
> *Marking Imaging Program*
> *Engineering Reliability Manager (retired)*
> *Xerox Corporation*
> *Webster, New York*

My Philosophy with Engineering

Engineering & management skills are always necessary to see complex projects through from conception to end. You can master a wealth of techniques both old and new for handling diverse requirements when a project engages many activities. Make sure you have the facts, real, certain, and actual, above all never second guess. Be sure to communicate with top managers about perplexing issues. That tactic will always pay off.

Communication skills are very important especially with your capability to listen, mediate conflicts and deal with various personalities.

You must also be ambitious; it is important to have the right attitude and be sincere. As an engineer or manager, be patient and friendly. Sometimes you may want to think differently — never go in that direction. Be forthright with the facts and be sensitive, especially when problems are complex at issue. When this happens be relaxed, strong-willed and being forthright with a positive approach, you will display great wisdom. I have often thought of this as the "Pioneering Spirit." If you are going to be persuasive, be very skillful with your presentation and know the facts. Above all, be loyal to your management and your friends will always be with you.

Keep in mind the need to develop strategies for prioritizing tasks. There is a need to analyze a projects cycle, however, my main concentration was with developing a *Timeline,* assigning tasks with a firm hand and keeping suppliers or participants on track. Nothing happens by itself.

Always be prepared with a back-up plan, sometimes a simple list of; "Item description - Subject & Predicate" will help. *Management* many times was surprised with the data I had available. You can easily rank projects or tasks by keeping the top priorities on a separate list for maximum effect and meeting tight deadlines with plenty of room to spare. Smart goals are always specific, motivating, and achievable with results driven and trackable.

All I wanted to do was honor, respect and revere *Xerox Corporation* with the early copiers, duplicators and printers that created a new way of producing copiers. This was a heyday for *Xerox Corporation.*

Putting the *Xerox shareholders* first was as important to me as everything in the *Introduction and My Philosophy with Engineering.* In the *Xerox Manufacturing Fabrication Engineering Office,* we were constantly reminded of the shareholders with a bell that rang at 10 am and 2 pm, the opening and closing of *Wall Street* and the price of *Xerox* stock. Keeping the *Xerox Shareholders* happy was one of my main objectives.

I sincerely hope in reading this book you may want to rethink and adjust your career. The one tool to lead to a better work life is opportunity. Tremendous success can be achieved; however, you must take the time and effort to always understand the facts.

I would like to take some time to briefly review some of the work ethics and the principles that will inspire you for a better work life.

Ethics and Principles Overview

Strategy:

As I mentioned earlier, communication skills are very important, especially with perplexing issues. Listen carefully and mediate conflicts or misunderstandings. Know the facts, real and certain and never second guess.

Be straight forward, use common sense and be sensitive and precise.

Optimism:

Always expect the best outcome with any circumstances. Consider the bright side, ultimately you will prevail. If you consider negatives, these may be turned into positives, but it may not be easy. Your colleagues will always be around when you are inspired and enthusiastic.

Timing:

Timing is always critical, and it is <u>everything.</u> If the timing isn't right, your efforts will be wasted. Plan carefully. When utilizing a Timeline, understand the details and never underestimate the liabilities.

Risk:

You must be willing to take that extra step if you are to be creative and effective. Make sure your "strategy" (first item in *Ethics and Principles Overview*) is on solid ground.

Respect:

Always treat another person in a way that shows understanding of their needs and rightness. Respect is an attitude that develops through mature and mutually enriching interpersonal relationships. Moreover, respect is the attitude of accepting others' differences.

Ambition:

If you have a strong desire for success you will need to apply extraordinary effort. Be prepared. Make sure you get plenty of rest.

Assertiveness:

Be confident, honest, and direct when claiming one's rights or putting forward your view. Having the quality of expressing your opinion or desire in a confident way, then management and your friends will take notice.

Savoir Faire:

The meaning is simple, "Saying the right words at the right time". You can influence management greatly and this will help your image.

Honesty / Trust:

Often data or information can be inaccurate and that will lead to a credibility issue. Being honest with trust and integrity leads to success.

Unity:

Learn to agree and work together. This quality will go a long way. Never disagree unless you are knowledgeable with the facts.

Vision:

From the very beginning of *Xerox Corporation* our founder *Joseph C. Wilson* wanted each of us to "inspire others" and to "attain personal goals". These factors will greatly influence your thinking and decisions.

Opportunity:

Just about everything in our life and career is an opportunity for advancement and to be successful. Thinking positive, you will be amazed at how successful you will become. I have always thought of opportunity as an enabler to *"Achieve your dreams"* and *"Invest in your future"*.

Perseverance:

Understand it is worth fighting for. If you strive to keep this high on your *Ethics List* the possibilities will be endless. Remember perseverance will always be a continued effort, despite obstacles or difficulties. Achieving success with steadfast perseverance will always happen with self-discipline.

Leadership:

Leading the way requires efforts to calmly confront the problems and understand the challenges, but do this with firmness, determination, and perseverance.

Patience:

You must have the ability to stay calm and accept delay with anything annoying, without complaining. This may be difficult, but staying calm with a little practice will go a long way.

Devotion:

Consider this as a strong attachment (I always put my employment with *Xerox Corporation* first). It can also be great love or caring for someone or something.

Praise:

Positive praise will always help inspire everyone for their commitment.

The bottom line is:

    1)   Communication is very important, that is what *Xerox Corporation's* philosophy has always been.

    2)   Create a vision and get others to accept and embrace it.

    3)   Greet everyone with a smile and say, "Hello or Good Morning," this will more than pave the way with favorable results. This in many ways will help establish your credibility with your coworkers and upper management.

Overall, my ethics, vision, and values would never change. Management recognized and appreciated how I navigated through difficult problems, with always the right outcome for *Xerox Corporation.*

Donald A. Drexler
    Marking Imaging Program
    Engineering Reliability Manager (retired)
    Xerox Corporation
    Webster, New York

Contents

Chapter I - Secretary of the week award

On a Wednesday in the spring of 1966, as I was driving to work, I heard an announcer say over *WHAM,* a 50,000-watt radio station that they were sponsoring a *"Secretary of the Week Award."* This would be held with their *Secretaries Week* during the following week. I thought this would be great for boosting the *Xerox Corporate* image. I wanted to nominate our secretary.

Dorothy (real name) was our department secretary, and my first thought was, could I pull this off? Since I was to be in Detroit on Friday for the *Ford Motor 100 Sportsman Event *,* I had little time to put this together. Obviously, I could not ask our secretary to type a letter recognizing herself.

A second problem was I was not to do any typing by overstepping the secretary's job. Also, our secretary *Dorothy* was very protective of her *IBM Selectric* typewriter. She told all of us that no one was to ever touch it. I did not have a good typewriter at home and hers was the best recourse. Now I have only one day to pull this off. I wanted to nominate our secretary for this award and the only way to accomplish this was to type it myself.

That evening, I started to put together everything I knew about *Dorothy.* I knew I would have to be selective from my massive notes.

For the good of *Xerox Corporation,* she strived to excel and that was also part of the *Xerox Pioneering Spirit.* She had a natural gift of writing and speaking. Friends would use her as a resource when seeking information. *Dorothy* pursued perfection and accuracy, her work with me was complex with *Engineering Technical Documents*. She always had an overwhelming desire to help. She was inspiring, displayed great wisdom, strived for harmony, and had a fun side evident in her dry wit. I could always count on her to do the job and she was very supportive of the other secretaries, at a moment's notice. *Dorothy* would initiate conversations with total strangers and her smile was enlightening and that made everyone feel warm and welcome. She had the ability to work well with engineers, other secretaries, and managers. *Dorothy* was dependable.

With all of this in mind and a handwritten draft, there was no opportunity to type this during the day.

The next day after 5:30 pm with no one around, I sat down at her desk, uncovered the typewriter, and tested the keyboard for touch. Now I was in trouble, *Dorothy* had the keys set for an extremely light touch. As I was typing I was double tripping the keys. It took me some time to adjust to her settings.

I started to type one page and decided to tear it up, putting the remnants in my pocket. When I was young, I was taught to "leave no trace behind"! So, I continued putting the nomination letter together paying close attention to my opening and closing paragraphs. I wanted to capture the radio station's attention. I started my opening paragraph with, "In these exigent times I would like to nominate" ... etc. I thought the body of the letter was well selected to obtain the best effectiveness. The last paragraph ended "as secretary she is an Olympic 10 out of 10." I was certain the last paragraph was sure to get the radio station's attention.

(Note my reference was using the best *Olympic Judges Rating* applied to work abilities.)

I drove directly to the *Rochester, N.Y., Main Post Office* that evening to make sure the nomination letter would be delivered in time.

On my way to work Monday morning, I was listening to *WHAM* radio, and I was pleasantly surprised, when they read my letter over the air. Our secretary *Dorothy* had won the *"Secretary of the Week Award."* During this announcement the radio station mentioned there were over a hundred powerful recommendations sent in.

There were many secretaries at *Dorothy's* desk that morning and a lot of excitement. What caught my attention was the vase of flowers that took up about half of the desk space. All I could think of now was impacting *Dorothy's* productivity with the company. I felt that I had overstepped my position, without question.

I was expecting censure or reproach that day, but nothing happened. The reason for the reproach was that I used a *Xerox Corporate* letterhead with a *Xerox Corporate* envelope without permission, however I paid the postage.

The letter being read over the air with radio station *WHAM*, certainly nurtured our name and likely inspired sales. Since this was all done in good faith, – then what could have been said to me? If there had been any statements directed to me by my manager, I would have countered with strong positive and firm statements, that would have been very difficult to reason against.

The radio station went all out with gifts such as a corsage, cut flowers in a vase, perfume, candy, theater tickets and much more. That first day *Dorothy* wanted me to pin the corsage on her, I politely shook my head "no." One of the other secretaries would surely do that. Each day *Dorothy* received something different. Each day was a new surprise. *Dorothy* became a very close friend.

I received numerous phone calls from managers and co-workers who said, "We should do more things like this to recognize good people." My immediate manager never said one word to me about what happened. I could say more, but this is about being caring and practical.

To be involved, inspiring and caring for other people is what it is all about.

I might add here that in 4 ½ years I never had to send an *Engineering Technical Document* back to be retyped. The typewriters then did not have memory.

I initially realized the letter to the radio station might be a long shot facing a very large number of candidates for the *"Secretary of the Week Award."* However, win or lose, I felt my actions might set an example for other engineers and managers to follow.

* I also won the *Ford Motor 100 Sportsman Event.*

"Striving and Excelling will always be part of my Pioneering Spirit at work and play."

Donald A. Drexler

Manufacturing Engineering Technician Manufacturing Engineering Standards Xerox Corporation

Chapter II - Scrapping of Excess Inventory –

Part I of II

Early summer 1969 I was working for *Manufacturing Standards* in the *Manufacturing / Fabrication Engineering Department* at our Webster, NY campus. I was walking by the shipping dock & noticed a Pull & Take Premier Scrap Company (P&T) flatbed truck (with extra axles). The P&T truck was loaded by our shipping dock personnel, with eight skids of (*Xerox code 09-1901*) polished stainless steel sheet stock with a blue plastic coating to protect the mirror finish. There was a handwritten sign *"Excess Inventory"* attached to one of the skids. Having a metrological background, I estimated the material weight to be 40,000+ pounds and an estimated cost of $100,000. My first thought was, we are using this material every day. Why is it on the P&T scrap truck? These special skids (4'x8') were placed by our shipping dock personnel on the flatbed at random, but not on top of each other. More than likely the fork truck driver had difficulty with the weight and pushed the skids to distribute the weight evenly. This scrap situation using the words *"Excess Inventory"* seemed to be an opportunity, into which I was drawn. I felt this was wrong. I needed a well thought out plan with a goal to prevent this from happening. Now being already engaged with these thoughts I asked myself, "Who knew about this and was it acknowledged by *Fabrication Engineering Leadership?*" I needed to be extremely careful and prudent with my thoughts, actions, and temper. Not knowing who may have authorized this process, I wanted to be incredibly careful when discussing the *"Excess Inventory"* situation.

In discussions with the shipping dock personnel, they stated: "This is happening daily." That was an honest response. Now, I am thinking there may be something else going on here, but I did not want to go in that direction.

To keep everything positive and being concerned about the tonnage and loss of this polished stainless steel, I decided to have a serious discussion with the *Manufacturing Fabrication Press Area supervisor*. I mentioned to the supervisor the stainless steel on the P&T flatbed truck. My approach was patience and perseverance, and I could not get him to realize the importance if we had a material stock outage, for production parts. His response was "If *Production Control* put a sign on the material that said, "*Excess Inventory*" they know what they are doing."

This was a losing battle; however, I was not giving up. I decided to go directly to *Production Control*. *Production Control* reports to *Procurement* in another division and not *Manufacturing Fabrication Management*. *Production Control* was scrapping material without *Manufacturing Fabrication* knowledge.

In confronting *Production Control*, I decided to keep my assertiveness at a lower level without creating a crisis yet being frank and straightforward. In trying to ferret out information on "*Excess Inventory*" activity they would not acknowledge ownership or what was happening. I was being stonewalled by *Production Control*. As I was asking questions, I was counting on facial and body language reactions. If the answers did not match the reflexes, I kept this to myself. The problem with "*Excess Inventory*" became bigger than I thought.

I then decided to go to my manager Kyle the *Standards Engineering Manager* for *Manufacturing Engineering & Fabrication*. When I informed Kyle of what was happening, he stated he did not believe me. My response was "Come with me and I will show you." I took him to the shipping dock, and I showed him what was on the P&T scrap flatbed truck with the sign on it- "Excess Inventory." The evidence then was believable and beyond debate. Kyle shook his head in concern and stated he would talk to *Production Control.*

The next morning, I spoke to Kyle, and I expected support to resolve what was happening. I did not see the support and I was sensitive enough not to ask why. If I had to say anything, it was like trying to put a dent in an 800-pound marshmallow. Suddenly that morning the P&T flatbread truck was gone. I let Kyle know. He didn't say anything, just shook his head back and forth, and it seemed neither of us could do anything.

I couldn't describe the sinking feeling. What else could I have done? I tried to think positively. That reminded me of one of the greatest musicals, *The Sound of Music,* and the final scene where the *Von Trapp* family are trying to escape. The Germans are in the chase car and all you hear is the starter cycling but the engine won't start. The next frame is a nun in habit stating to her Mother Superior "I have sinned." Her Superior said, "And what is that sin?" The response from the nun was to lift her hands, then present her with the distributor cap and the spark plug wiring harness. I could have only wished to do something like this, but I know that would not have been representing my style.

Two days later, Charles the buyer for raw material stainless steel sheet came into my office very disturbed. Charles had the ability to be understanding and be patient. However, he was not comfortable or at ease with me as he stated, "You scrapped my stainless steel." I then said, "What are you talking about?" He replied, "You scrapped the stainless steel 09-1901 material, and the lead time to get more was 16 weeks." I stated, "I tried to stop the P&T scrap company from getting it." I also advised him, "I told my manager Kyle, who also tried to stop it." I wanted to get Charles to settle down and I offered him a cup of coffee. He accepted. We engaged in excellent conversation with efforts to resolve what was happening. Because of a 16-week lead time we were without the stainless steel 09-1901 to produce several parts. Charles would be contacting all the US steel manufacturers (*Bethlehem, Republic, US Steel* etc..) to locate some inventory to keep *Manufacturing Fabrication* from shutting down. Charles managed this crisis by getting some of Stainless Steel 09-1901 from all over the United States, at a cost I don't want to talk about. Charles was also aware *Production Control* reported to *Procurement* (in his own division). Two and a half weeks went by and neither Kyle nor I could accomplish anything. During that time, I had conversations about the cost regarding "Excess Inventory" with Johan – *The Manufacturing Fabrication Plant Manager*. He was concerned with raw material / inventory loss getting out of control. Returning to my office, I noticed *"Suggestion Forms"* at the *Xerox Document Center.* I took one to my office and started to write up what was happening with the "Excess Inventory." I was trying to be practical and positive and was using the wrong words. Well, I went back, took a second form, and again said the wrong words. My determination and patience prevailed with a good 3rd suggestion draft. Part of this suggestion was to place inventory elsewhere off-site if necessary. This suggestion would be responded to by a *Xerox Vice-President of Marketing,* located on the 13th floor at *Midtown Plaza* in *Rochester, New York.*

Let me give you some insight into what was happening. The *Xerox Manufacturing Fabrication (XMF)* plant produced parts for the 914, 720, 813 and 2400 copiers. *Production Control* who reports to *Procurement,* did not have space in *(XMF)* Building 208 to put raw material or parts. Calling material "Excess Inventory" was an easy way for *Production Control* to get rid of it.

I showed the draft to Kyle, my manager. He reviewed it and stated, "We could not go in this direction." My response to him was "Then we are part of the problem." He did not have to think twice about my response and said, "Send It." I slept on it overnight, polished it up the next morning, had it typed and sent. A week and a half later I received the suggestion response from the *Xerox VP*. In his second paragraph he said, "This is not happening." I read it twice in disbelief. I made a copy of that letter and gave it to Kyle my *Engineering Manager*. Kyle came up out of his chair and said, "What's the matter with this guy? Is he out of his tree?" My response was, "Kyle, settle down and let me try to talk to him." All day long, about every 45 minutes I called the VP, and I could not get to the inside secretary. I was talking to the outside secretary about every 45 minutes. This secretary was the *Vice President's* perimeter defense. I could not get to the inside secretary. Finally, late that afternoon at 10 minutes before 6:00, I called again, and I was talking to the inside secretary. She said, "He is here, let me put him on." To make the story short, I informed him of what was happening, and that I could get him paperwork and samples to prove what was happening and he agreed. The next day I advised my manager of the agreement.

I wanted to refocus on my goals, plan carefully and keep my effort and commitment positive. Creativity would be important. However, it was evident that there would be risks associated. Could I develop a different and brilliant approach? This was an opportunity I had to approach with persistence and leadership.

You will find my approach and the results in Chapter 2, Part II of Excess Inventory.

"Persistence and leadership will always pay off when resolving problems."

Donald A. Drexler

Manufacturing Engineering Technician
Manufacturing Engineering Standards
Xerox Corporation

Donald A. Drexler

Chapter III - Scrapping of Excess Inventory -

Part II of II

The combination of circumstances of failure with the previous chapter, where nothing could be accomplished, it was obvious my support was limited to Johan, the *Fabrication Engineering Plant Manager.* In Chapter II part 1, I mentioned Johan, but I didn't say I also knew his wife and family prior to joining *Xerox Corporation.* Johan was a brilliant manager and if I approached him with the right attitude, I would gain his support.

I worked for Kyle in the *Manufacturing Standards Fabrication Engineering Department* for approximately 4 ½ years. All those years I received excellent reviews and basically maxed out in my pay grade. Kyle knew, I never left a stone unturned. I was entrusted to write accurate and precise machine specifications along with procedures. That was my primary objective. My manager was very skillful, and I needed to be sensitive with him with any approach to resolve the "Excess Inventory" discarded material. The reason for this was simple; Kyle, in discussions with *Production Control,* could do nothing to suppress or overcome what was going on. Also, the words "Excess Inventory" were not in any part of my job description.

I could not accomplish anything with the discarded material; therefore, I was orphaned. I needed to plan very carefully. My approach would be deliberate and tactful with communication aimed directly at achieving the end results with Johan.

My manager Kyle had already approached *Production Control* and he was unable to resolve this situation. I did not want to overstep authority. This was simply a case of "darned if you do and darned if you don't!"

Because no one knew who authorized this activity, I felt the idea of upsetting a nest of wasps was not good for the company or myself. Evident risks would be associated with this if I discussed this with the wrong people. I would need to maintain good communications with the top plant *Manufacturing Fabrication Engineering Manager* – Johan.

Communications is what made Xerox Corporation great.

In light conversations with Johan I mentioned, "If I had the opportunity to act, someone more than likely would want me fired." Johan's response was "Do it, I will take care of that at my end." With firing being cleared up, I now have license to move forward. Johan also mentioned he was "losing too much inventory." I also mentioned I had witnessed outbound "lined" cargo containers, that could very well be sporadic escapes of "Excess Inventory." If the cargo containers were lined, then more than likely good material was in them. I would have to investigate this a bit more closely.

I wanted to be enthusiastic about this, but my position at *Xerox Corporation*, writing standards for *Manufacturing Fabrication Engineering,* both for equipment and processes was very important. I also felt that if my manager Kyle knew that I was looking into the "Excess Inventory" scrap problem, he would say nothing to me. With that in mind I suspect when he initially approached *Production Control,* he was likely told, "To back off, it's not your problem." Now the only time I could devote to this problem was during my lunch hour or after work. Could my persistence ever pay off? Less than a week after the polished stainless steel disappeared, there was another special skid on the shipping dock. This special skid was 8' long with 2 – 6" x 6" timbers supporting it at the base. This special skid would not fit into the *Hartman Racks* or the *Kenway Inventory System* because it was too long. Loaded on this special skid was 14,000 pounds of screws. These were mostly small machine screws of many various sizes, with hex-nuts and washers for assembly production. I tried to guess how many screws there would be in 7 tons. Forget it. This special skid was next to some cargo containers, and with a sign "Excess Inventory," this sign was buried and out of sight. I would never have noticed the sign if I wasn't inquisitive. My next immediate thought was to control my blood pressure.

Apparently, *Production Control* did not want to break this skid down and put the material on normal skids. This would take too much of their time. Normal skids (3'x4') would fit into the *Hartman Racks* or the *Kenway Inventory Storage System*. I needed to initiate an action plan to deal with the current affairs of *Production Control* and to adjust my suspenders.

First: I needed to place a "Hold Tag" on this special skid, and it was not to be moved for 48 hours. The hold tag was immediately filled out and placed on the skid.

Second: In conversations with the dock personnel this skid was not to be moved and special paperwork would be forthcoming.

Third: I needed a small box to get a sample of some of the screws. The dock union person was very courteous and cordial and stated he could get a sample for me, and no one would ever know he was in the skid supply box.

Fourth: I am in a *"Free Trade Zone"* controlled by *U.S. Customs*, and I needed special paperwork with plenty of signatures to send a sample of screws to the *Vice President of Marketing*. This is well documented toward the end of Chapter II, Part 1 of 2, where I agreed to send samples and paperwork to the *Vice President of Marketing*. Note: The P&T scrap company could take it away without any paperwork. However, to send a sample to the *Vice President of Marketing,* I was required to make sure it was authorized by the top personnel in our *Manufacturing Fabrication Engineering Plant*.

Fifth: I would only inform top management of my activity. I let Johan know that all hell was going to break loose. He smiled. With the small box of screw samples, I talked to my manager Kyle, and I stated I needed special paperwork to send the screws to the *Vice President of Marketing.*

The next morning our secretary approached me and asked if I needed this special document. My response was "Yes, and I am going to get fired today." She stood there for about 30 seconds, said nothing and, I did not say anything more. She finally left, I then reached into my desk drawer, grabbed the scotch tape, rubber cement, staple gun, the document, and I immediately left for the shipping dock. I rubber cemented the document to the top box on the skid, stapled it, and scotch taped it well. A dock union employee came over as I was removing the "Hold Tag" and asked what I was doing. My response was "sending this to the *Vice President of Marketing.*" He looked at the paperwork and said, "You're sending 14,000 pounds of screws to the *Vice President of Marketing.*" My response was "Yes." I won't even try to describe his reaction.

The plan is to have a truck capable of transporting at least 7 tons to be at the shipping dock at 9:30 am. At 9:30 am there was still no sign of a heavy truck. A little later a trucker with a fork truck drove in to pick up the screws. The trucker slid his forks under the skid and raised the forks bringing his rear wheels off the ground about 5 inches. What happened was the furthest point on the skid was the heaviest load. The trucker releveled the fork truck and then repositioned the heavy load by hand closer to the fork truck, to achieve the center of gravity. My next reaction to this was, "Where is a bigger truck?" He was heading toward the ramp and the only truck was a panel truck about 20' long. He moved the skid down the ramp and immediately the truck bottomed out on its springs and shocks. I suspected the tow motor operator was not aware of what happened. The truck immediately left. Later that day there was a P&T scrap company truck identical to the truck that took the stainless steel that drove off unfortunately empty. I would like to refer to this as, "just in time."

This load would be delivered to *Midtown Tower in Rochester*, where the *Vice President of Marketing* was located. Now riggers would be involved to get this load to the 13th Floor. When riggers accept an assignment, they have a commitment to overcome anything that is challenging. The first problem is the skid weight is 14,000 pounds and the elevator maximum weight is 5 tons. Therefore, this load will have to be split up, putting it on two regular, heavy-duty skids. You might say this is accomplishment number 1. These skids will then later fit into the *Hartman Racks* or the *Kenway Inventory Storage System (back in Webster)*. The paperwork with this assignment clearly stated to deliver this to the *Vice President of Marketing's* office on the 13th floor at *Midtown Tower in Rochester*. When riggers have clear instructions, they do just that and will not leave anything in the aisle or passageway. Riggers have a very strict bond amongst themselves to follow instructions carefully. The *Vice President of Marketing* was furious with me and wanted me fired. I tried to think of this for him in a positive way, he did not like the two skids, which I referred to as *"End Tables"* that really upset his decor. By capturing his attention, I was sure this approach would come back through the "chain-of command." It sure did. I had to paint this kind of picture to accomplish the end results. I expected "all hell would break loose." That was exactly what I planned.

Later that morning, just before lunch, my manager Kyle saw me from 80 feet away and he was coming at me like a sidewinder missile. He approached me with a very reddish complexion and asked, "Did you send a skid of screws to the *Vice President of Marketing?*" It was obvious he was in distress. My job endurance was on the line, but not my leadership ability to resolve problems. I paused in thought and lifted my thumb and index finger to my jaw and very calmly said, "Yes, you signed the paperwork." I could see he was overwhelmed by this statement, knowing at the same time his manager Johan supported my commitment to save tens of thousands of dollars in inventory. My manager Kyle did not say anything, just turned and walked away.

This activity triggered a phone call to *Production Control,* and I advised them to get the 14,000 pounds of screws out of the *Vice-President of Marketing's* office at *Midtown Tower in Rochester* on the 13th floor. Then get them back to *Webster Manufacturing Assembly* for inventory. I simply stated they needed to act immediately or there would be "fireworks."

That afternoon about 2:00 pm I was trying to relax and getting a cup of coffee from the *American Restaurant Association (ARA)* coffee machine when the *Plant Manager* Johan saw me and busted out laughing. In the process, he put his hand on my shoulder and lightly stated, "the *Vice President of Marketing* can get rid of the screws by taking a handful every day and drop them down the mail-chute." Of course, this was all fun, and I enjoyed the humor. I mentioned to him I had already informed *Production Control* of what they had to do. Within the next five weeks I had over one hundred phone calls asking, "Did I really send a skid of screws to the *Vice President of Marketing?*" The answer was always, "Yes – I had to paint that kind of picture to get the end results."

Six months later at the *Webster Manufacturing Complex,* we had over 90 tractor trailers packed with inventory in the parking lot. We had space problems without question.

It was hard to imagine the amount of time required to retrieve a truck, then obtain the parts required, and then repack the truck. This was all part of growing pains, and the *Excess Inventory* problem (of scrapping good material) was resolved.

"If you are involved, you will always make the World a Better Place."

Donald A. Drexler

Manufacturing Engineering Technician
Manufacturing Engineering Standards
Xerox Corporation

Donald A. Drexler

Chapter IV - THE XEROX MANAGEMENT

ASSOCIATION

I joined the *Xerox Management Association (XMA)* in 1970 as a *Charter Member*. The *XMA* was formed by a group of managers, inventors, and scientists. I was very much impressed with what they offered. The people that were signing up for membership were highly talented and very committed to *Xerox Corporation*. The *Xerox Management Association* wanted to help, develop, and promote the wellbeing of the *Xerox* image.

The social aspects were unity, companionship, and fostering recreation, travel, and amusement. Meetings and fashionable dinners were well planned with brilliant people. They cultivated good taste, embraced a warm welcome and always rendered respect along with politeness.

Initially the dinner meetings were planned for members only. Eventual meetings included wives or significant others. If your wife or significant other came in formal dress, she would not be out of style.

This culture and its virtues riveted my attention. This certainly was an attractive draw. The principles they stood for reflected what I wanted. This would contribute as a channel to being a better person.

I was amazed with what they were doing and never anticipated my endeavors would capture their attention, my being an engineer among a group of brilliant scientists and inventors. I was credited as being a radical and a devoted engineer. It was this style that caught the attention of one of the *XMA* managers.

While at the monthly meetings, I met Thomas, a manager with *Xerox Customer Relations at Xerox Square, Rochester, New York*. He was self-motivated, had a refined way of communicating and had a finesse for getting things done. I admired his "radical style," and our friendship grew.

At one of the early dinners, *Mr. Irving Wermont* was requested to give a talk on *"Memory and Concentration."* I knew of him and would not miss his talk. There were 550 managers, scientists, and engineers signed up. On arriving at the front entrance, he was there greeting each person. He would ask you your name and ask you to take a playing card (he had about twenty decks of playing cards in a box). Then, he would ask you what card you had before he marked a number on the back of his business card. Before handing you his business card he said, "If we ever meet again, tell me this number and I will tell you your name, where we met and what playing card, I gave you." During his talk on *Memory and Concentration,* he took out five magazines he picked up at the airport and read on his flight to *Rochester, NY*. He then passed them out to the audience and said, "Tear a page out and tell me the magazine name and page number and I will tell you what was on that page." A hand went up and a person said, *"Mr. Wermont,* you could have access to pre-released magazines." *Mr. Wermont* replied, "I will get back to you. Please stand up and remain standing."

When the magazines were distributed and pages removed by the audience, he began asking people to raise their hand and tell him the magazine and page number. As each hand went up, he went into detail of what was on that page, who they were and what playing card they had in their pocket. After about 20 pages, people stopped putting their hand up. *Mr. Wermont* then said, "I have here a bank draft for $1,000.^{00}. If there is someone here, I do not know, please come up and claim this check. To the person that was still standing, he said, "I would like to introduce you to everyone here. As I call each person, please remain standing after I call your name." He called off the first person's name that was standing, then continued with the names of the management at the *Party House*, delivery people, restaurant staff and waitresses in attendance. Then, he began by naming all of the people at the rear tables working clockwise around each of them and doing each row before moving forward to the next row of tables until everyone was standing. I didn't think the applause would ever stop.

I will never forget that night. I also remembered *Mr. Harry Lorayne who did a similar demonstration on the Ed Sullivan Show* back in the late *1950s and the 1960s.*

- -

My friend Thomas, with *Customer Relations* at *Xerox Midtown,* called me one day and said he had tickets for an *XMA Dinner event,* and he wanted my wife *Philomena* and I to attend. I was working long hours and stated I would try to attend. Thomas was insistent that my wife and I be there. Thomas worked with *Xerox* customers, and he could accomplish almost anything. He was a genius at getting results. Both of us had parallel courses for meeting a goal. However, there was always more fun in his methods. Initially I did not pick up on this, however, he mentioned my wife first and not I.

We had a good sense of humor, and I never gave it a thought that he would take advantage of me.

Then my wife could not make one of the meetings. This was noticed by Thomas. I received a phone call and Thomas requested; I bring my wife to the next *XMA* dinner meeting. I am not quite sure, but I suspected this festivity would be entertaining. I also suspected the entertainment / recognition, would be focused on me. I informed my wife to "be prepared" for whatever recognition was coming my way.

Thomas happened to be seated at my table for that dinner. Then it was his turn to speak at the podium to the audience. He began to talk about how I accomplished results. There was so much laughter from the audience I began to wonder, "Where are we going with this?" Then he requested I come forward for something special. I looked at my wife and said, "Honey, hang on, I don't know where I am going with this."

Arriving at the podium, I was to be recognized for some of my accomplishments. The next thing you know I was being handed a package which was about 2 feet by 3 feet and a couple of inches thick wrapped in the "Sunday Comic pages." I immediately guessed I was going to be roasted.

Thomas handed me the package with an entertaining smile and said, "Open it." I didn't want to open it, and that drew laughter when I nodded my head "No way."

Removing the "Sunday Funnies" and shaking my head again drew more laughter.

I decided to look at the Sunday Comic wrapping, well that drew laughter.

Next, I'm looking at a framed poster about 36 x 28 inches of a laid-back orangutan monkey with the slogan, *"Just when I knew all the answers, they changed the question."* I said, "I would cherish this." Those in attendance just busted out with laughter.

They wanted me to hang it in my office. My response, was "No Way." Shaking my head back and forth drew more laughter.

With a serious look, I said, "This is really fashionable." Folks again, busted out with laughter.

I finally said, "I will keep up appearances with this."

Again, everyone just busted out with laughter and applause. They also loved my instant reactions and the approach with the *"Give and Take."*

Why I Wasn't Fired at Xerox

If there was ever a festive and enjoyable time, it was that evening.

- -

Everything was going fine for months, with the *Xerox Management Association*, then I received a call from Thomas, and he wanted me to go on a trip to *New York City*.

I mentioned to him, "My platter is overloaded, and I am sorry, but I have to decline."

The next thing he said was, "No, you have to go."

My response to that was, "Thomas, you are in a different division with *Customer Relations at Xerox Square, in Rochester* and I work with the *Xerox Manufacturing Division in Webster, New York*. Besides, I don't report to your division."

His response was, "No, you are going, both of our *Xerox Vice Presidents* are aware of this, and the airline tickets are in the mail, you will have them this afternoon." There was no question, this was a deliberate move.

To make it short, I went to the meeting in *New York* and came back as *Vice President of the Consumer Groups of New York*. My responsibilities grew exponentially. Now, I had to rethink everything, however my responsibilities with my position at *Xerox* would be first.

I had to keep a polished image, embrace a new itinerary and with good humor make someone laugh occasionally. I cherished this, but it was not easy.

The monthly *Xerox Management Association* meetings were well attended, I cherished these meetings. I would take my wife to dinner and if she wore a very nice but simple evening dress, she was not out of place. My wife enjoyed these events and the warmth that made her at ease. These people were *"The Best of the Best"* and were from all walks of life.

Etiquette, fellowship, and fashion were only what you could dream about. Savoir faire is defined as knowledge of what to do or say and when or how to say it. The *XMA* meetings were held with savoir faire!

"I always liked a small amount of humor that kept me from becoming overly serious."

Donald A. Drexler

Manufacturing Fabrication Engineer
Manufacturing Fabrication Division
Xerox Corporation

Xerox 2400 Class Picture
Class Picture from the Drexler Gallery

The book's author Don Drexler is the engineer in the back row
near the center with a bow tie.

Chapter V - A Learning Curve

In the late 1960s I was developing organic (paint) specifications for all the *Xerox* finished machines. Working closely with the *Manufacturing Finishing Manager* George, I developed a very positive relationship. I was very appreciative of his support for my common-sense measures and conservative principles. George also knew I had a metallurgical background, and I realized my background would fit very well in his department. I kept all of this to myself.

While writing standards for Kyle my *Fabrication Manufacturing Engineering Standards Manager,* I would always approach the manager of each department *(Milling, Drilling, Welding, Plating, Finishing, Gage Inspection and Tool Room)* of that section to ensure my work was accurate and concise prior to publication. I could adapt to almost any situation and part of my philosophy was to never overstep anyone. *Xerox Corporation* had codes, written and unwritten, that adhered to basic common sense. Now suddenly, my image was going to be in jeopardy. One of the codes was "engineers and managers were to wear white shirts and a tie." Well, to make the story short, I got up one morning and all my white shirts were in the wash. The only shirt available was a light-yellow dress shirt. I realized I would be approached by my manager and the conversation would not be good. There would be no way to get out of this using a skillful tactic, I would have to resort to humor. Sure enough, my manager asked why I had a light-yellow shirt on? My response was "My wife doesn't like to use bleach." That statement didn't help the situation. I offered to go to a local store and purchase a white shirt. My manager said, "No, but have a white shirt tomorrow." Two days later several engineers were wearing light blue, green or pink shirts. Two weeks later about 25% of the engineers were wearing light-colored shirts. At that same time, one of my co-workers said to me "Thank you for changing the atmosphere." My response was "It happened by accident." This change became well cherished and created a "more at home" friendly environment.

In referring to a friendly environment, I worked with an inorganic engineer named Franklin who was black and was always willing to support your undertaking. He was brilliant in his field of work and if anyone could be a close friend, it was him. Then one day during Yom Kippur he was wearing a skull cap, I liked him even more. Two weeks later while at his desk he started to sing "How Great Thou Art." He was singing at an upper-level tone that was magnificent and beautiful. He sang three verses, everyone in the engineering office stopped working, stood up, applauded, and said, "More, more!!" What "a friend to have," I should underscore the word _"friend."_ Having a black Jewish engineer who could sing a Christian hymn with such a beautiful voice gave us pause to consider the wonderful gifts and talents from God amongst us.

In working with *Fabrication Manufacturing Engineering Standards*, I was required to spend considerable time for data development within the *Metallurgical Engineering Department.* These engineers were highly talented with brilliant leadership abilities. I often thought that a career in this field would be good and then talking to one of the engineers he was planning on quitting the company. He was tired of doing the same thing over and over. He became a *Division Plant Manager* of a very large industrial manufacturer. Another engineer took the *Vice President*'s position with *Xerox Marketing*. I was then convinced I would cherish this work. However, I wanted to undertake a position as a *Manufacturing Engineer* resolving problems or trouble shooting. I had no idea what was waiting for me down the road.

Why I Wasn't Fired at Xerox

While working with the *Metallurgical Engineers*, there was a simple case of – something was needed but lacking and fun would be the answer. While having metallurgical conversations with one of the engineers, suddenly, a small speaker system in the *Metallurgical Engineering Department* announced, "Now hear this, battle stations, battle stations!" Everybody, including the person I was talking to, jumped up to do something and I had no idea of what was happening. The person I was talking to said to me, "I have an assignment." I still had no idea of what was going on. Everyone was hurrying to put something together. It was a long chute with an incline of about 3 feet and loaded with a torpedo on wheels. Over the speaker, next were the words" Five, four, three, two, one, fire!" The torpedo went down the chute, travelled down a small aisle very fast toward the main aisle.

In the main aisle there were many people going in both directions. My first thought was someone was going to be hit with the torpedo. My second thought was "should I be associating with these guys?!" The distance from the chute to the main aisle was about 35 feet. The next thing I see is one of the *Metallurgical Engineers,* Harold, walking in the main aisle, towing a battleship on wheels with a string. The torpedo made a direct hit. Over the speaker system then were the words, "Battleship destroyed!" Then someone said, "Back to work." This all happened in about twenty seconds. This moment of fun was captured in my memory forever, but then I wondered how I might be involved in the next prank.

A few weeks later I was required to be on the production floor near heavy equipment. The equipment used heavyweight soluble oil. Not far away was a rack of parts, and I heard a breaking noise, I could not move fast enough. The rack broke and the parts went into the soluble oil, a brown color. (I referred to this as babysh*t.) I was drenched with the oil, even being ten feet away. I needed to get to my manager and let him know what happened. On the way to my manager, I had to go by the *Metallurgical Department* and one of the engineers Harold saw me and said he could start up one of the heat-treating furnaces to dry my clothes. There were wash basins in the lab, to remove the soluble oil. I mentioned I needed to first talk to my manager. In talking to my manager, I stated if I were to go home it would take at least one and a half hours. I mentioned the option to clean up in the *Metallurgical Laboratory*, he thought that option was viable and would save time. In the *Metallurgical Laboratory*, Harold (the same person who towed the battleship) fired up the heat-treating furnace and put a metal rack in front of the furnace about 3 feet away.

Meanwhile, I was in a white lab coat that didn't fit and didn't even cover my knees. There was so much oil in my shirt and trousers I could not spot clean. It was difficult getting the oil out of my clothes. I positioned my clothes on the rack and after about five minutes I had to move the rack further away (now over 5 feet) from the furnace because of the intense heat, my trousers would have been burnt toast. Because of Harold's determined persistence in helping me, I decided to relocate myself to another part of the laboratory, where counters and cabinets would just help to protect my image. Then I decided to move some equipment, to barricade myself for a little more privacy. This was done because Harold left the lab swiftly. One of my tendencies (my sixth sense) was to read into this. I suspected there was some underlying action going on! Sure enough, the next thing that happened was all the secretaries were taking a sudden tour of the *Metallurgical Laboratory*. My pants were the center of attention. The secretaries did not know who they belonged to. Thank you, dear Lord, for my sixth sense. Soon I was back working like nothing happened.

Why I Wasn't Fired at Xerox

*"You can always have fun, but try
not to be the Center of Attention."*

Donald A. Drexler

*Manufacturing Fabrication Engineer
Manufacturing Fabrication Division
Xerox Corporation*

Donald A. Drexler

Chapter VI - Multiple Challenges

In the summer of 1969, *Xerox Corporation* was growing rapidly. We were building the last of the floor model *Copier 914*. Another version, the model *720*, was setting the world on fire and sometimes itself. Customers didn't mind a fire now and then. The important matter was that it produced lots of copies. Another smaller *Desktop Copier, the 813* went into production in October 1963. The latter was referred to as a desktop copier and it weighed 190 pounds. Two riggers would have their hands full placing it in an office. Along with all this excitement and busyness the next generation model, a *Xerox 2400*, was at the beginning of the production stage. As I pointed out in *Chapter II and III*, we struggled with storage room for raw material, parts, and inventory.

With all this happening, I knew there were prosperous times ahead. The future of *Xerox Corporation* was looking bright, or at least we had the outlook of a successful future. A primary objective involved staffing engineers, managers, and union personnel. We needed unity and positivity to inspire the workers. We needed to be sensitive to the workers' thoughts, ideas, and feelings. It seemed like unity should be an overall objective.

I would like to quote *Charles R. Swindoll* who said, "Life is 10% of what happens to you, and 90% of how you react to it." I couldn't come upon a better commitment for *Xerox Corporation*. I would always try to do my best to honor what was expected of me and try to take risks.

My next surprise was the *Manufacturing Fabrication Engineering Finishing Manager* – George requested that I transfer to work for him. I responded with a "Yes, I'm sure you have plenty of work for me." His response was "I need you."

George was most certainly aware of, what I stood for, and I would honor his requests.

I knew that George had been looking for a smart, creative, innovative person. He needed someone who could follow *Xerox Policy* but also think outside the box. He needed a "Type A" work-ethic engineer and a multi-tasker. There were a lot of projects to juggle at one time. He also wanted a person whose integrity would not be compromised. Because of my past achievements, I was that person.

When it came to *Xerox Policy*, yes, I sometimes would bend the rules. However, I knew if it came to union regulations, I would have to adjust my activities to obtain the end results. You might say "I was a risk taker." It didn't make any difference who you were, a manager or an engineer… my ultimate loyalty was to the *Xerox* shareholders. If you were to stand in my way (figuratively), I would verbally respond that "you should be very careful."

George oversaw *Organic Finishing (paints), Inorganic Finishing (plating), Injection Molders (plastic), Metal Finishing, Welding and Plasma Spray.* My flexibility would be stretched even further. I was determined with a positive attitude to overcome any challenge.

My introduction to this group of engineers was very cordial and inspiring. I felt I could support almost all their endeavors. However, I did realize a need to focus on some production problems in the welding area. Part of my responsibility was to be effective with union personnel. In my mind one of the keys to effectiveness is to be good-natured. I needed to be positive and praise the good things that were being accomplished, to inspire workers along with management for their commitment to their work. Unquestionably, *Joe Wilson* was the best at this.

On day #2, the first thing I did was to plan with the *Senior Welding Engineer* – Walter to investigate numerous problems in the welding area. After a fifteen-minute discussion, it was agreed I should reach out to Carmine the foreman in that area for his input. I wanted to be supportive, and I recognized my approach needed to be gentle if I was to fit in. I introduced myself to the *Welding Foreman* - Carmine and mentioned I was available to support him in my role as an engineer, and that I could resolve some sensitive problems. He said my commitment was very praiseworthy and he was appreciative of my help. He acknowledged there were some personnel problems, but only elaborated on one instance that *Engineering, Management and Production* would need to be reviewed. He was waiting for a meeting to discuss this issue with Walter the *Senior Welding Engineer*. Some preliminary meetings happened but nothing led to resolution.

I realized why I was brought on board. I needed to be tactful and delicate with those involved and I needed a better understanding of the situation. I figured I needed to wait for the *Senior Welding Engineer* to talk to me.

The First Challenge:

Finally, Walter the *Senior Welding Engineer* came to me and said there are serious personal problems with the *Amalgamated Clothing and Textile Workers Union* personnel in the *Fabrication Welding Area*. We needed to discuss this behind closed doors. Four trips were made to the *Fabrication Welding Area* to verify settings with the *Projection Welding Equipment* for hold and squeeze times. Of these four trips fourteen jobs were found running out of process. It was strongly felt the hold and squeeze times were cut, so the operator had a way to make the rate. I initially felt the *Time Study Department* production rates were off with <u>effort</u> and <u>skill</u>. The data included date and time of check, machine number, part number, operation number, part name, with required and actual hold / squeeze times.

Some of the variations that took place that would cause weld failures are as follows:

Squeeze Time: a) Premature firing, b) Firing with inadequate pressure, c) Improper clamping prior to flow of current, d) Increased electrode deterioration and e) Excess weld flash.

Hold Time: a) Inadequate cooling of weld, b) Sheet separation due to forces being relieved before total solidification and c) Increased electrode maintenance due to improper cooling after duration of current flow.

I signed a letter about the above, which was cosigned by the *Senior Welding Engineer* and sent to Nathen our *Fabrication Welding Manager* with copies to the *Fabrication Production Managers*. I would have thought this letter would have caused a reaction from the union workers.

After a few weeks the *Amalgamated Clothing and Textile Workers Union* workers were not complying with hold and squeeze times as spelled out with the *Fabrication Welding Process Instructions*.

The "next step" would be to install locked panel boxes on all *Projection Welding Equipment* controls. Or another option would be to have *Manufacturing Welding Engineering* farm out all *Fabrication Welding Processes* to suppliers that were qualified. If this were to happen many *Amalgamated Clothing and Textile Workers Union* workers in the *Fabrication Welding Area* would be out of a job.

The word leaked out and I was getting phone calls from buyers, they were ready to start sending assemblies and parts for immediate welding.

My response to the buyers was, "We have not pulled the plug yet... *Xerox Procurement* is not to take any action without *Xerox Fabrication Welding Engineering* management approval.

Suddenly the *Amalgamated Clothing and Textile Workers Union* workers were complying with *Xerox Fabrication Welding Process Instructions*.

The Second Challenge:

Another problem in Carmine's *Metal Finishing Area* was that the engineers in welding and finishing could not get the *Time Study Department* to respond to inquiries. I introduced myself to a young man named Alex, a union person in the *Metal Finishing Area* and he showed me what was required to finish a panel. I made a quick estimate of the time for the entire process. The *Job Time Sheet* timing (estimated by the *Time Study Department*) wasn't anywhere near the actual time. I asked Alex if there were any more similar panels available for another test. There were none in the immediate area, but Alex told me of two-part numbers that had do-able production time. Each run was normally only about 100 panels for painting and assembly. This was limited because of storage space. I looked at Alex's finished work. It was excellent. The corners were perfectly rounded and there were no visible signs of welding. I praised him for his superior work and stated I would follow up with him the next day.

Immediately I headed to the *Time Standards Department* and spoke to Bill the manager. He referred me to Kenneth. I requested the *Job Time Study* data from Kenneth. The folder he retrieved had no supporting data, just initials written next to the times. I questioned why we had an actual time on the production instructions. Kenneth had no answer. I told Kenneth I was going to break the rules to resolve this problem and that I would need his help the next morning. That afternoon I requested three panel prints. I did a quick visual study of surface preparation, the number of linear inches to be finished and compared that to the panel without data. With some quick math in my head, I came up with an estimate for a standard time that was only slightly more than what I had recorded with my watch with Alex. This was a bonus because Alex's performance was greater than 100% efficiency (output divided by input). I also did a percentage calculation, and I was surprised how close that was.

The math in my head, with the above story reminds me of a schoolteacher who disliked my approach. I worked on the math problems the way my father taught me, so I received zeros on my quizzes even though my final answer was correct. She thought I was a problem child. However, for the *New York State Regency Exam*, only the answer mattered. A few days after the *Regency Exam*, my teacher announced each name and their score. She started with the highest score and worked down to those that flunked. As she was reading down the list, I began to worry at not hearing my name. I was certain that I had at least half of the answers perfect and felt pretty good about the rest. Finally, she said "Let's talk about *Don Drexler's* test." It took three exam judges to look at it and all three agreed I didn't push hard enough for one period. That was all she could get me on. I received *National Honors*. Let's get back to the Time Study.

The next morning, I was back with Kenneth in the *Time Study Department*, and I gave him all my math except the efficiency rating including the marked-up prints. I requested he establish a *Time Standard* for the panel in question and he obliged me. With the new *Time Study* results I went to Carmine (*Metal Finishing foreman*) who asked, "How did you do this?" I just smiled and said, "It was no problem." I was able to calculate realistic time standards and that was beneficial to the workers. I became friends with Alex and his union co-workers. They liked me even more when I bought them all coffee a few days later.

Getting the result of this assignment, you won't find my process in the manual.

Kenneth worked for *Time Study* for another year before he was offered an excellent position with *Production Control*. His manager warned him if he left and took the other position, he could never come back to the *Time Study Department*.

He took the position and a year later the *Time Study Manager* retired. Guess who took over the manager's position. That's right, Kenneth. Way to go.

"Being smart, creative, and innovative is only part of being an Engineer. You must also be accurate and precise."

Donald A. Drexler

Manufacturing Fabrication Engineer
Manufacturing Fabrication Division
Xerox Corporation

Donald A. Drexler

Chapter VII - Unleashing a Radical Engineer

When I resolved the *Time Standard* problem in the *Metal Finishing* area, it caught the attention of the foreman Carmine in the *Welding & Metal Finishing Area*. Since I reached out to help, he was determined to keep me involved with some other issues in his area. I figured there were two realistic reasons for this.

First, *Time Study* was overwhelmed with work and shortcuts with personnel were not working to their benefit.

Second, *Metal Finishing* was part of the *Welding Engineers* responsibilities, and the *Welding Engineers* were swamped with near constant problem calls leaving little time to focus on the *Engineering* objectives.

Time Study was not part of a *Metal Finishing Engineers* job description. Therefore, it took second place to the normal process. Or to put it more simply, it fell through the cracks. Years later the *Process or Manufacturing Engineers* would be required to establish production rates. *Xerox Corporation Management* would teach the course, "*Methods, Time, and Motion (MTM)."* I disliked the motion part of the course. I felt I could evaluate efficiency better with the stopwatch and be fair with job rates, for the *Amalgamated Clothing and Textile Workers Union* personnel.

Working with Carmine it was evident I needed him to recognize my commitment to equipment and processes, not personnel issues. He understood my boundary lines.

The following is a synopsis or condensation of events that transpired with the last production run of side panels for the *813 Desktop Copier – Line Out* situation.

1)　　My phone rang at 5:45 pm. The *Welding Foreman* Carmine was in big trouble and *Production Control* was all over him. We were about to build the last of the *813 Desktop Copiers* and we required 190 side panels for the *Production Line.* We had none.

2)　　The *Welding Fixture* had been broken because a forklift truck ran over it 6 weeks earlier.

3)　　The *Punch Press* area was setting up a press and keeping senior workers on overtime to get the job done.

4)　　The *Welding and Metal Finishing* area was doing the same including inspection.

5)　　The game plan called for side panels in the *Painting Department* at 7:00 am the next morning. The *Painting Department* had a chain driven serpentine conveyor about 1,200 feet long which did everything. Workers needed to only load and unload special racks for the panel painting. This equipment automatically electrostatically painted the parts (both sides) and baked the finish in about 1 hour.

6)　　About 8:00 am the panels would be delivered to the assembly line. After final run and test, the machines would be ready for shipment. This was an all-out effort for everyone.

7)　　I called my wife *Philomena* immediately and apologized that I would not be home for supper. I would grab a snack from the break area. She understood I was dealing with a major problem. My wife was a saint in adjusting her schedule and she understood my work dedication.

8)　　Normally, I had an arsenal of personnel that was available but not necessarily after 6:00 pm. I put together a quick common-sense plan in my head. This might be a time to NOT put something on paper.

9)   I headed straight for the *Xerox Tool Room*. Although there were only a few workers there, I knew one who was highly skilled, and I felt I might be able to convince his supervisor to lend me a worker.

10)   I spoke to the supervisor about what was necessary. He looked up the *Welding Fixture* number and stated the *Tool Room* had repaired the fixture and sent it to the *Metrology Gage Lab* about two weeks earlier.

11)   I headed off to the *Metrology Gage Lab* and the foreman Keith (also known by other engineers as Caesar) looked up the *Welding Fixture* number and said, "I don't have it!" I explained when the fixture was released from the *Xerox Tool Room* and sent to his *Metrology Gage Lab* for inspection.

12)   Again, he replied, "I don't have it!" Other engineers warned me that some people in the *Metrology Gage Lab* "played games." Others referred to them as "Prima donnas." They were the only inspectors that wore long white lab coats. I knew I needed to be tactful with the supervisor, I politely asked once again if he was sure he did not have it. He began to get annoyed and responded, "How many times do I have to say, "We don't have it!" I nodded my head slightly, accepting what he was saying and left.

13)   I advised Carmine in the *Welding Area* of what transpired and let him know I was not done yet.

14)   I went over to *Production Control* and there was no one around. Finally, I found a manager out on the floor. He was aware of the *813 Desktop Copier – Line Out* problem but not the fixture problem.

15)   He suggested we go over to *Crib #4* – they have good records. We went there and it was locked up.

16)   We then went over to his office, looked up the phone number of the person with the crib key and was able to retrieve a key.

17)   With key in hand, we went to the crib and in the records there, discovered the fixture <u>was</u> <u>sent</u> to the *Metrology Gage Lab* on the same day it was received by the *Tool Room*. (This *Welding Fixture* was then sitting in the *Metrology Gage Lab* for two weeks.)

18)   I then asked the manager to check the *Tool Room* rack in the crib. The *Welding Fixture* I was looking for, was not there.

19)   I returned to the *Metrology Gage Lab* and waited for the supervisor to get off a long phone call. I told him I needed his support, and I could see he was irritated with me.

20)   I needed to turn the conversation around so he would not be totally ticked off. I stayed calm in explaining the situation, but his reactions were not positive. I felt like I was interrupting his quiet time. Again, he stated, "We don't have it!"

21)   I asked to see where tooling was received from the *Tool Room*. From his reaction I could see I was in unfriendly waters.

22)   He took me over to the storage area and stood directly in front of the fixture while facing me and stated again, "We don't have it!" He was offended by my insistence, and he showed it.

23)   I knew what the fixture looked like, I just pointed to the welding fixture <u>directly</u> <u>behind</u> <u>him</u>, where he was standing. His resentment, displeasure, and irritation of me remained. I knew now what

other engineers were saying about personnel in the *Metrology Gage Lab.*

24)   There was a print with the fixture that was marked up with *Tool Room* calculations.

25)   I marked up one dimension and "I requested that I needed only that one dimension verified." This was something that could be done with calipers in less than a minute, although paperwork would take longer.

26)   There were at least five inspectors working in the *Metrology Gage Lab* and any one of them could have completed this task in less than five minutes.

27)   The supervisor said he didn't have a person available now, but he knew about the situation on the *813 Desktop Copier - Line Out* problem.

28)   He said right after break at 8:00 pm he would put a person on it.

29)   I agreed and left. When I returned to the *Metrology Gage Lab* at 8:15 pm there was no one around.

30)   At 9:00 pm the supervisor came back. Two people in his area are working but neither on my *Welding Fixture.*

31)   I again asked for help, but he said he couldn't do anything until his people were back from the *Clean Room.*

32)   At 9:30 pm I decided to go to the *Clean Room,* to see what was more important than the *813 Desktop Copier - Line Out* problem.

33)   The *Clean Room* door was locked. From a nearby window, I could see what looked like the three inspectors to be at a table playing cards. I was tempted to get security and another foreman involved, in breaking up the party.

34) I knew if I did that, I might still lose an opportunity to get the panels finished in time for the *813 Desktop Copier* - production line.

35) I decided to bite the bullet and play their game.

36) A little after 10:00 pm, the three inspectors are back in the *Metrology Gage Lab* and one of them has my fixture set up on a *Rand Surface Plate*. While he was taking dimensions, I would not disturb him.

37) However, they would clock out at 11:00 pm. They also would clean up about five minutes before that.

38) I decided to arrive a little before cleanup and went straight to the supervisor.

39) As I entered the *Metrology Gage Lab*, I noticed my fixture was still set up on the *Rand Surface Plate,* but no one was around the set-up doing anything.

40) I went over to the *Metrology Gage Lab foreman,* and he already had his coat on at his desk. I asked the supervisor if the weld fixture inspection was done, and he said, "yes."

41) I then asked if it was done, then, "How come it is still set up on the *Rand Surface Plate?"* I did not get a response; I then requested a copy of the *Metrology Gage Inspection Report.*

42) He got his keys out of his pocket, unlocked his desk, removed the report from his locked desk drawer, and handed it to me.

43) I noticed it was not signed by the inspector.

44) The Metrology Gage Lab foreman then took the report back and signed it himself.

45) I then took the report and marked on it *"Pending Line Trial"* and gave the supervisor his copy and kept mine.

46)   When I turned around all the *Metrology Gage Lab* inspectors were gone.

47)   Then I said to the supervisor that I needed that fixture in the *Welding Department* to produce panels and the foreman there was still paying senior worker's overtime.

48)   He said, "Take It." As I reached to unclamp the fixture, I heard a voice say, "I'm not done with that."

49)   I turned toward the voice and because he was sitting on a highchair, I could only see his shoes beneath a *Jones and Lamson* wall curtain.

50)   I felt the inspector was hiding there waiting for me to do something so he could write me up. This was a setup.

I didn't respond to his con game. I put the fixture under my arm and walked away heading to the *Welding Department.* As I was walking, I pondered what had transpired between 5:45 pm and 11:00 pm. Everything with the *Metrology Gage Lab* was delayed. The *Metrology Gage Lab* supervisor and the *Amalgamated Clothing and Textile Workers Union* inspectors were forcing me to act so they could file a *Union Grievance* against me.

At that time of night, human resources were not available to witness any exploitation. Even though there was an *813 Desktop Copier - Line Out condition* which required immediate action without delay, there were still intentional delays in the *Metrology Gage Lab*. When the *Metrology Gage Lab* supervisor had his coat on, and his desk was locked up, it was obvious that he did not care if there was an *813 Desktop Copier - Line Out* condition.

I felt his action was deliberate especially after he retrieved the unsigned *Metrology Gage Inspection Report* from his locked desk. The *Production* people were on double time (by *Amalgamated Clothing and Textile Workers Union* rule) and being paid for waiting around most of the evening. Further delay would inflict additional heavy cost. Common sense was to expedite matters without further delay.

In the *Welding Department,* I found one dimension was .040 inches short. It was a difficult dimension to measure without special tools. Being short, we rigged the fixture with shims and duct tape for this final run of *813 Desktop Copiers* produced at the *Webster, New York* complex.

It should be noted that further delay would have been devastating and that would have inflicted higher costs. Common sense was to expedite this matter without further cost. I was not about to spend a small fortune or more delays for tooling that would only be used once. All tooling after this production run, for the *813 Desktop Copier* would be delivered to a refurbishing center in *Oakbrook, Illinois*.

Carmine and I worked on the fixture with scrap parts until we got it right. Shortly after 1:00 am we were producing perfect parts. The panels then had to go to the *Metal Finishing Department and Inspection*, be cleaned and then sent to the *Painting Department* to be painted when that line opened at 7:00 am.

I stayed until about 2:30 am. I arrived home at 3:20 am, I climbed into bed without waking my wife. I overslept that morning and arrived very late (about 11:00 am) at work. A co-worker asked, "Where were you this morning?" I truthfully answered, "Out on the *Production Floor*." Before he could say anything else, I added, "Ask Carmine the *Welding Foreman*."

The next three months were relatively calm except for some behavioral problems in the *Welding Area* which was not part of my responsibility.

Each year the *Amalgamated Clothing and Textile Workers Union* had more demands. Most of their demands were outrageous and beyond debate. It was obvious the Union did not understand the word, "Unity."

Xerox Management was typically ready to cooperate if that would influence or improve working conditions and productivity. It appeared to me the union wanted more than they needed. (Of course, what happened to me, was a set-up that would expose their actions). I could never understand why they would do things like this. In the end they would poison themselves. Years later when the *Fabrication Manufacturing Plants* shut down, that ended many good paying positions.

Three months later this event will come back to life, and all hell will break loose. Continued in Chapter IX.

"Being an Engineer, you must be committed
to your company, policies, and procedures."

Donald A. Drexler

Manufacturing Fabrication Engineer
Manufacturing Fabrication Division
Xerox Corporation

Donald A. Drexler

Chapter VIII - A "SMALL" BEHAVIORAL

PROBLEM & SOME EDUCATIONAL

ADJUSTMENTS

Now it's back to the *Engineering* in the *Welding & Metal Finishing Department* with everything running smoothly. Carmine the foreman for those two departments thanked me for the support with the side panel for the *813 Desktop copier.*

Next, I began studying to acquire more knowledge of projection welding. My only knowledge was with *Stick or Metal Inert Gas (MIG),* welding. Walter the *Senior Engineer* was state certified in every type of welding including *Sub-Mergeable Arc Welding.* Finally, I acquired knowledge to do regular welding set-ups. The next thing you know, I was being primed (taught a crash course) with inorganic finishing with Franklin the *Inorganic Chemical Engineer.* I did not want to get involved with the chemical principles. This was a very large and specialized field. That stated, I was now more in control of my destiny. I hoped. A couple of days later I was approached by my manager George. I could see he was in deep thought, he motioned me to come over closer to his office before he mentioned to me, "You will be responsible for the *Plasma Spray Equipment.*" What a relief this was. I was expecting to hear about the fixture I tore down in the gage lab described in the previous *Chapter VII, "Unleashing a Radical Engineer."* I began to think, "What is happening with the *Plasma Spray Equipment?"* The only thing that came to mind, was the book titled *"All quiet on the Western Front."*

The *Senior Engineer* - Walter came to my office and said, "We need to talk." He usually had a smile. This time there was no smile, and he was serious. My first thought was "What did I do now?" I made room for him to sit down in my office and cleared off part of my desk. My sixth sense anticipated that whatever this was, it was not going to be good. I offered to get him a cup of coffee and he declined. After searching for words, he finally said, "We have a massive problem in the *Welding Area*." My response was "How can I help you?" He then went into the details. Again, the *Spot-Welding* operators were reducing the time in the set-up and apparently that was causing welding failures. I asked if this involved more than one operator. Without pause Walter said, "I think it is all of them." In further discussions it was revealed that if the operators saw him in the area, they would reset the hold and squeeze time to the proper settings. He suspected that there was even an audible signal to other operators by dropping a tote pan. We needed to act, but it would be difficult to prove they tampered with the settings. This was a nightmare.

The *Welding Foreman* Carmine could not get control of the situation. Carmine said he needed to have a conversation with me. I asked Walter if he needed to bring Jake (a *Senior Foreman*) into the conversation and his reply was, "No, not yet…This was an *Engineering Problem*, and we need to take more steps to resolve it." Walter did his best to encourage good workmanship but since that was not working, he wanted (me) the new kid on the block to be used as an ice breaker. My first thought was the devil is all over the place. How am I going to orchestrate this one? It was evident I was in this deep. I also felt this was a huge opportunity that would enable me to achieve success, or I was being set up as a scapegoat. I wanted to know if the times or rates to run the various jobs in the *Welding Department* were fair. I was looking for a reaction. There was no body language in his response just "I believe they are." Eventually I took stopwatch readings from my trousers pocket and confirmed the timing rates were good. I needed to verify that prior to my approach to the *Time Study Department*. The *Time Study Department* was now out of this entirely. I suspected the conditions in the *Welding Department* were going to lead to little cooperation with the union operators. Should I influence upper management to act? This would be a last resort.

I felt as a *Welding Engineer* we had the leverage to overcome this situation with a letter to management and the union which in part would state:

> Production time for set-ups on all welding equipment was not to be changed.

or

> We would install a locked clear cover over the welding control panel, that only the *Welding Foreman* or *Welding Engineer* had access to.

also

> *Manufacturing Engineering Management* would have the option to farm out all welding to the best bidder.

I planned a letter with the *Senior Welding Engineer* that would be sent to *Engineering Management, Production*, the *Amalgamated Clothing and Textile Workers Union* and *Buyer Management*. I can only say if this got out, there would be a lot of calls from the buying community which would be premature to pursue bids. That did happen. My response to them was very firmly stated, "We have important options first, before we pull any plug."

With this letter there was a lot of cooperation. In *Production Control & Procurement* only a few of the people there knew me. Because of that and top management involved, I knew I had some leverage with control. It's always nice to know if you fire a warning shot that is strong and tactful, you can get reasonable results. The *Senior Welding Engineer* and I could not have ever conceived of a better plan.

Meanwhile everything on the *Production Floor* was running very well. The *Plasma Spray* unit was running flawlessly. This process sprays (like spray painting) a very thick liquified molten aluminum onto a surface to be machined later. For its time it was a *"State of the Art"* process and part of the process was proprietary and I will say no more at this point.

Just prior to my vacation of 2 weeks during plant shutdown, I did a quick inventory of materials required for production to resume. We were in excellent shape. When I returned after vacation ended, I entered the engineering office main aisle, and my manager George was forty feet away looking me in the eyes (not good) and standing with his arms folded in front of him. I approached him and said, "Good Morning." He replied with, "Where were you at 7:00 am?" I responded, "Having breakfast with my wife." He knew I always put family first, so that lowered the heat a little. He said, "Your *Plasma Spray* is down." My response was "I will get on it." The foreman in that area was aware we had fifty-nine miles of aluminum wire available prior to shut down. There was none to be found. Other engineers from my Manager's *Fabrication Engineering Area* looked all over the production plant and could find nothing. They even checked the shipping docks. I was reminded of the *"Scrap Excess Inventory"* problem and hoped this was not connected. I even climbed up cargo containers for inspection and some were four containers high. I needed to take a break, I was tired and therefore I decided to wander over to the *Plasma Spray Equipment Area*. Upon close examination of the feeder, I could see a very short piece of wire protruding. The wire had been cut with a pair of wire cutters. A short distance away was an unloading section at ground level used by the *Plasma Section* along with *Xerox Maintenance* for heavy weight material or material that required careful handling. The missing wire was special in that a small kink or nick could interrupt the coating process resulting in scrap. The lead time to obtain more wire was about 8 weeks at best. My conclusion was that the wire was probably stolen. I immediately touched base with the buyer. On mentioning what I found with my manager George, I could see his reaction, and only describe it as a sinking feeling. He said, "Get a hold of the buyer." I told him I already did, and I offered to obtain up to six miles of wire at a time and bring it back to *Xerox*. Also, I knew we had enough inventory of plasma sprayed parts to keep our copiers going out the doors for five weeks. The buyer obtained wire in less than three weeks. We were able to adjust without major problems. Later that fall, just after Thanksgiving, a theft ring in *Xerox Maintenance* was broken up. Several people involved had high paying *Xerox* jobs, and I could not fathom why they would do something like this.

Not long after that, my manager wanted to see me. On entering his office, he said, "Close the door and pull up a chair." Nevertheless, I did that and said, "How can I help you?" His response was, "You have to go to school." All I could think was, where is he going with this? He then said, "I'm sending you to school in *Connecticut* to bring you, *"Up to Date"* with the latest *Plastic Injection Techniques and* everything is paid for." I recognized this was another opportunity to expand my knowledge in the manufacturing world.

I did not understand why I was selected, there were engineers in the plastic field that were way more knowledgeable with plastics, and I thought they would be more beneficial to *Xerox Corporation* in the long run. I then considered what *Xerox Corporation* always wanted, creativity, outside the box thinking, sometimes radical pathways to get to the result. They also looked for people who were deeply involved with the company. I was honored that *Xerox* selected me for the *"State of the Art"* learning.

These classes were inspiring and would influence an investment in me for the *Xerox Corporation* future. The only problem was the school scheduling. The education was non-stop and challenging at times, I would regularly call home each evening about 7:00 pm and talk to my wife, each night I would write up class notes for many hours until about 10:30 pm and put them in a binder for a report when I returned. Almost every night there was partying which I skipped, except for one weekend. Every morning, we were up at 5:30 am and the classes were fast moving. I was very appreciative of what *Xerox Corporation* was doing for me and I would return with an arsenal of knowledge that would benefit the company for years to come.

On returning to work, I presented the notebook I prepared while at school to my manager. The information captured my manager's attention. He said he was astonished at what I had put together. He did not expect to see an in-depth report as to the way I issued it. His response was, "This is an excellent accounting of advanced techniques with plastic injection."

I thanked him for the educational opportunity that expanded my knowledge in the current *"State of the Art"* methods with Plastic Injection.

"Never miss an opportunity to expand your knowledge, especially if you want to be creative."

Donald A. Drexler

Manufacturing Fabrication Engineer
Manufacturing Fabrication Division
Xerox Corporation

Chapter IX - All of a Sudden All Hell is About

to Break Loose

While entering my office, the *Senior Welding Engineer,* Walter stopped me, minus his usual smile. I could detect he was showing a strain. He asked if I tore down a fixture in the *Metrology Gage Lab.* Now, I knew that sooner or later that was going to hit the fan. I looked him straight in the eye with a puzzled look on my face, raised my thumb and index finger to my chin and stated, *"Come to think of it I did."* He almost fell apart before stating that George my *Manufacturing Fabrication Engineering Manager* wanted to see me. I stated, "I would see him immediately." He said, "No, don't go in there right now." My reply was "I have no problem explaining, so he understands my position."

On entering my manager's office, I could see he was upset. He quickly stated, "Close the door and sit down." After a few seconds he stated the *Amalgamated Clothing and Textile Workers Union* had a huge grievance against me and he wanted to know what happened. I informed him this happened over three months ago, and I had an event breakdown of what happened.

The synopsis of events can be found in Chapter VII:

It all started at 5:45pm as I was about to leave for home with no one else in the engineering office and ended at 3:20 am the next morning. This was an *Emergency Tooling* situation.

My manager listened very carefully without interruption and then gave me a lecture about company policies and procedures for ten minutes. When he finished, he said, "Do you have anything to say?" I just wanted him to hear my point of view and stated, "If I had to do it over, I would have taken the same approach as I did the first time."

I then received a second dissertation on *Xerox Corporation Policy and Procedure*. At this point (during his discussion) I thought I would interject something, because I always liked a small amount of humor that kept me from becoming overly serious. So, I said "If I need a jury, I want 12 *Xerox* stockholders." Based on his reaction I could see the short fuse was burning quickly.

Another lecture started and within 30 seconds I said, "George I know what you want me to say- that I was wrong." He cut me off and said, "Don't say another word" and he left the office.

I went back to work and about 20 minutes later was required to be on the *Production Floor* in the *Welding Department*. In the process I had to pass the *Metrology Gage Lab* and I noticed my manager giving a dissertation and chewing out to about 18 lab inspectors all in their lab coats. I didn't bother to stop.

Three days later two inspectors from the *Metrology Gage Lab* stopped me on the *Production Floor* and asked who I worked for. I mentioned George's name and I immediately detected a sense of unease. I somewhat anticipated this reaction. There was no justifiable way for the *Amalgamated Clothing and Textile Workers Union* inspectors to react to a lecture from George and if I had to say it, it was the beginning of the end for them. The two inspectors told me the *Amalgamated Clothing and Textile Workers* paid the $2000 + grievance out of their union funds to make the matter go away. That word spread quickly among the union production workers with some disdain for the other union workers involved. My image was now better protected, and I was one to be reckoned with.

Why I Wasn't Fired at Xerox

My manager and I had an excellent relationship and we both developed our talents to firmly communicate, especially with the *Amalgamated Clothing and Textile Workers Union.*

During the next three months, I noticed a more positive attitude on the production floor. I made more friends on the production floor. They were good-natured and appreciative of me just stopping by to say "hello" or "good morning." Cooperation and unity with the *Production Foreman* was at its best. Problems just seemed to disappear.

Suddenly, George wanted to see me. When I entered his office and saw the look on his face, I knew there was trouble. Again, he asked me to close the door and pull up a chair. He looked me straight in the face and said, "I'm in trouble." I kept my reaction to myself and listened not knowing what this was about. He then said, "I'm losing you." My first thought was that I was being put out on the curb.

He continued that William our *Manufacturing Fabrication Vice President* selected another engineer and I to resolve problems in the *Photoreceptor Division.* Our *Vice President* William had reviewed all *Engineering History* backgrounds of all those in the *Manufacturing and Fabrication* areas. Our *Vice President* selected my history because I had a metallurgical background and problem solving. The other engineer was selected for his forty years of machining experience. The two of us were to immediately meet with Peter, a manager in the *Photoreceptor Division.* I hardly had time to say good-bye to my co-workers. For George, my manager, that was a sad day. I wished him well and I hoped to see him in the future.

*"It will always payoff to have an
excellent relationship with your manager."*

Donald A. Drexler

*Manufacturing Fabrication Engineer
Manufacturing Fabrication Division
Xerox Corporation*

Chapter X - The Diamonds

On arriving at the *Photoreceptor Process Engineering Plant*, Fritz (the other *Fabrication Engineer* selected by William the *Vice President of the Manufacturing Fabrication Engineering Plant*) and I met with the *Photoreceptor Process Engineering* manager Peter. This was a very welcoming and cordial meeting and I felt very comfortable with him. There was no question he was very firm, and his primary objective was to get the lathe department up and running. This was his major focus because production was at 10% or below in the *Photoreceptor Process Lathe Department*.

I could fit in with Peter because he was inspiring, very quiet in a sense and professional. He seemed to be very forward, however I detected he was <u>not</u> <u>getting</u> <u>the</u> <u>proper</u> <u>process</u> <u>support</u> with the *Engineering Photoreceptor Lathe Department*. I felt there was a fundamental integrity problem also present. I needed to be very careful with my communications. Fritz and I were to report directly to Peter. Peter then asked, "When could we start?" My response was, "Immediately." Peter had already set up office space and phones for us. We were introduced to the secretary and were advised, anything we needed she would get for us. The last item Peter mentioned was the schedule. Could we cover a sixteen-hour workday between the two of us and possibly more? A second shift fits in with Fritz perfectly. Any schedule problems we would work out between ourselves.

The next step was we were to introduce ourselves to the other managers and to the *Photoreceptor Production Engineers* and Robert the *Photoreceptor Production Foreman*.

On arriving on the *Photoreceptor Production* floor, we immediately introduced ourselves to the *Photoreceptor Production Foremen*. In reaching out to them, we mentioned we were there to resolve problems, to work closely with them and to foster unity with everyone. I was surprised by one foreman's reaction; he hadn't heard the words, "Getting along with each other," in a long time. He showed appreciation for our support.

In reviewing the *Photoreceptor Production* floor situation, I needed to step gently in, especially with the *Photoreceptor Production Engineers*. Initially, I needed to navigate carefully with them, but at the same time, I could not overstate the importance of why I was there. I was there at the direction of my *Manufacturing Fabrication Engineering Vice President.*

The next day, all production lathes were down and only one person Albert - knew how to set the diamonds with the photoreceptor lathe turning process. He was not having any success with the machine set-ups. Occasionally, he would get a machine up and running but only for a short period. He was constantly jumping from one machine to another, to obtain some production. I understood the procedure well for setting the diamonds, however, I was not there for that purpose, I was there to resolve the problem. The diamond setting was not a science, but an art, to obtain a certain finish.

The excessive speed of over 9000 feet per minute and the diamond contact point (primary land or cutting/burnishing edge) created massive pressure on the diamonds. I believed Ulysses the *Photoreceptor Production Engineer* did not understand this.

The *Photoreceptor Production Engineers* had the *Xerox Maintenance Department* tearing the production lathes apart, looking at the headstock bearings and races, finding nothing wrong. I mentioned to the *Photoreceptor Production Engineers* including Ulysses, that before taking a machine apart they should do an *"Oil Analysis"* or at least a *"Patch Test."* They looked at me, as if I was interfering with their work and I was not playing by their rules. I kept this to myself, but the

Photoreceptor Production Engineers were stubborn at their best.

Years before, I worked in the aeronautics field, with hydraulics for the *X15,* the first fixed wing aircraft that went into outer space. We measured all wear in parts (metal in oil) in parts per million. If anything was to go wrong, we knew about it well in advance.

I could not get the *Photoreceptor Production Engineers or Engineering Management to* accept this thinking. I stated that I believed the diamonds in the tool holders were loose because of the <u>massive</u> <u>pressure</u> between the diamond primary land (burnishing) and the photoreceptor surface. No one in the *Photoreceptor Production Lathe Area* or the *Photoreceptor Production Engineers* would accept this. Fritz was a genius in the machining field, and thought they were loose from the pressure.

Every day I would meet with Fritz to go over everything and the conditions in the *Photoreceptor Production Lathe Area* were eroding worse than ever. Fritz mentioned he had some discussions with an engineer (unknown title) by the name of Ramon and was told, "When Fritz made his reports, he was to send a copy to Ramon, to our manager Peter and <u>no</u> <u>one</u> <u>else.</u>" (Now there seemed to be a cover-up). I was spending about 90% of my time in the *Photoreceptor Production Lathe Area* and never saw Ramon there once. Besides that, I was told I was to report to Peter.

Ramon was not in our organization chart, and I did not know who he reported to.

In discussions with another *Photoreceptor Production Lathe Engineer,* I had to say, "Before I would go any further, let me make a very important point, that I was here for resolution of the diamond turning process, and not for someone else's agenda." I did not see his cooperation.

I needed a lengthy discussion with Fritz. In doing so, we covered a lot of what was going on. I had to question the philosophy of our treatment. All I could think of was, "We are outsiders and not part of the good old boys club." There seemed to be concealment within the *Lathe Area Operation,* and we had to play by their rules. Both Fritz and I were tolerant and could somewhat adjust to the oppression that was going on. I felt the impact on our individual mental and physical health could be profound if we didn't get a handle on it. With this statement we needed to balance burnout. One thought was, "Could we break the rules?" Since we did not have cooperation – should we go directly to Warren the *Photoreceptor Vice President?* With that thought, we decided the risk and benefit was not worth it. We decided on better conditions to support the *Photoreceptor Production Lathe Engineer* and to foster getting along. We needed to establish trust and unity. Both of us would support any measure that would inspire *Photoreceptor Plant Management.* Conditions in the *Photoreceptor Production Lathe Area* were not good and every minute mattered.

As I mentioned earlier, I felt the diamonds were loose. When I say loose, that is one to three, ten thousands of an inch (or .00010" to .00030"). That is so small, it is very difficult to measure without special equipment. It's like splitting a hair 30 times.

I was using a microscope in the *Photoreceptor Production Lathe Area* at 800 power to review the cutting surfaces with top rake and the primary clearances and found only <u>circumstantial detail</u> that would not affect the diamond finish that was required.

Two weeks passed and I was now dedicating time with the microscope (800 power) to look through the diamond at the backside mounting surface for any sign of movement. Regardless of what I did I could not detect any movement mechanically.

Why I Wasn't Fired at Xerox

At **3:15 am** one morning, Robert one of the *Photoreceptor Production Lathe Area Foreman* stopped by and said, "Don, you look tired, let's get a cup of coffee." My response was a slow but sure, "Yes." Just before Robert stopped by, I had placed a diamond that could not achieve a finish, in the microscope holder. I was adjusting the microscope lens to look at the back side of the diamond mounting surface. We used a very light penetrating fluid for a coolant, and the diamond was well exposed to the fluid. I had just moved a 5-watt Christmas light over close to the diamond so I could see through the diamond, to the back side. We went for coffee.

Ten minutes later I returned, looked in the microscope and I could see the coolant at the back side of the diamond (at the mounting surface) was moving slightly. This was because of the heat generated from the Christmas light bulb. I reached up and touched the diamond with my fingernail, and what I saw, if I could explain it was like; "The inside of a Maytag Washer in action."

I finally proved the diamonds ♦ were loose.

I again estimated the looseness was .00010 inch to .00030 inch.

I advised the *Photoreceptor Production Lathe Area Foreman* and wrote this up for my manager with a copy to Fritz. Then I decided to go home at 4:15 am and get some sleep without waking the wife.

At 9:00 am, I woke up and decided to go to work to follow up with my findings.

Arriving late at 10:30 am that morning, I decided to go straight to the *Photoreceptor Production Lathe Area.*

The *Photoreceptor Production Lathe Engineer* set up two *Bunsen Burners* under three feet of gutter pipe, heating the cutting fluid. The cutting fluid was very flammable. This was done to heat the diamonds in their holders, and then verify with the microscope (800 power) the diamond back side for

81

looseness. Any detected fluid movement, the diamond(s) were loose and required re-brazing and re-sharpening.

I requested they shut this down immediately and put it in a clean room with plenty of air flow. The response was, "We're okay and we have a fire extinguisher here." I responded, "Shut this down immediately, I don't want people getting sick from an exchange of gases with other cleaning solutions, and an open flame." I had to assert authority which was very effective when I mentioned the exchange of gases. I did this to focus on safety and at the same time foster a way to get along and be good natured about it. The set up was immediately removed from the *Photoreceptor Production Lathe Area* and placed in a *Clean Room* with plenty of air flow.

Most all the diamonds were loose in their settings. I called the buyer and found he had just switched to a new supplier, Best Tool Supply in Maryland. Using a light solvent with heat to wick around the diamond provided a process to verify acceptable cutting / burnishing diamonds. The microscope at 800 power was also required, remember we were viewing the movement of a light fluid (with a small amount of heat) within a space of one ten thousandth of an inch. The *Photoreceptor Lathe Department* foremen were very happy to get some production back to normal. The *Photoreceptor Lathe Department Engineers* never showed gratitude for resolving their problem, of course I am the outsider working in their area. The buyer was aware of a production critical situation with diamonds. I offered to drive to Maryland to bring back acceptable diamonds. I realized if brazing with the diamond was not properly done, they would not work. That's why I was utilizing the microscope (800 power).

Best Tool Supply had no experience with sharpening diamond cutting tools, so they sent some of their people to the Greater Tool Works in Maine, to find out how they were refurbishing the diamonds. The Greater Tool Works did not know, because their refurbishing Tool Maker retired on his 80th birthday. They convinced the company to share his name and address. Upon looking him up, he was not willing to share his secret method. He finally accepted a bank check for $10,000.^{00}. After depositing the check, he took them to the Greater Tool Works for a "Show and Tell" process. All he did was to put the diamond in its holder, in a vise and reflow the braze with an acetylene torch. A little braze may be added and then "finish grind" the cutting edge.

When the *Xerox Buyer* told me the above story, I was overwhelmed with joy for this 80-year-old Tool Maker. The feeling I had for him would remain with me forever. I was so glad he received an additional "retirement package" (call it what you want) for himself and his wife.

The bottom line is.

"Getting along with everyone
is a major key to success."

Donald A. Drexler

Photoreceptor Project Engineer
Photoreceptor Division
Xerox Corporation

Donald A. Drexler

Chapter XI - Installation of Precision Diamond

Turning Equipment

After resolving the lathe problem with loose diamonds, opportunities vanished, because I had no goals to focus on. This was demoralizing and I wanted to be committed to the company. I decided to try influencing Peter the *Photoreceptor Process Engineering* manager with the thought of improving cooperation in the *Photoreceptor Production Area.* I only thought of this, because of the past comments and oppression that was prevalent in Chapter X. I needed a careful conversation with Peter, which would expose sensitive situations, and I wanted to remain cautious yet be straight forward.

Suddenly, Peter came into my office and said, "Can you come over to my office? We need to talk." I went immediately to Peter's office. Peter closed the door and said, "I have a project for you." I stated, "Shoot." He then stated he would like me to install a photoreceptor lathe from the *Seneca Falls Machine Company* that would produce extra-long photoreceptors. I said, "No problem, and I know the managers in maintenance very well." My sixth sense just kicked in and it was evident he wanted me to take the path forward, bringing this special equipment into *Xerox.* I cherished this as a *Project Manager* and felt joyous with some normal working hours. I just hoped I would not be working at 3:00 am on problems as in the earlier chapter. Thank you, dear Lord, for giving me more time with my family.

Knowing Peter as being firm, steadfast, and resolute, the question came to mind; How come I was selected over other *Photoreceptor Engineers*? I suspected he was looking for someone like me who was firm, straight forward and handled sensitive situations very carefully. I also knew he was <u>not</u> <u>getting</u> the <u>proper</u> <u>engineering</u> <u>process</u> <u>support</u> with the *Photoreceptor Lathe Department.*

In discussions with Peter, he basically stated, to do whatever was required, and he was very professional about it.

My major focus would be to get a unique designer (for the machine base) on board immediately. Special skills would be required with diamond finishes, this would require understanding vibrations or shock waves. I knew I would not find these skills on hundreds of job applications. I would have to guide the designer. The one request Peter made was that the machine had to have a cast iron base. This was an excellent decision for controlling shock waves.

At the same time, I needed to establish *a Timeline,* obtain machine drawings, develop special tooling, including a special balancer and make sure I was communicating with the *Xerox buyer* and *Xerox Maintenance Management* almost daily or as required.

I did not like the proposed location for the new special lathe in the *Photoreceptor Lathe Department.* This location was close to an outer wall and fork trucks traversed over the concrete floor with wide joints or seams. This is now another problem. I decided to get a cup of coffee and place it on a 5-gallon empty bucket where the new special lathe would be placed. I sat down on a chair next to the bucket and watched the tidal waves in the coffee cup, caused by the fork trucks hitting the floor joint. I needed to isolate the entire concrete machine base from the production floor, because of the fork trucks hitting the joint or seam in the floor. *Kinetic shocks* would be the answer.

I was about three weeks into the *Timeline* (total plan) of just about seven months and a designer was now on board. Then, I received a call from the buyer, and he stated, "Can we bring the *Seneca Falls* lathe in, three months early?"

My response to that was, "I don't know, until I replan the *Timeline* with *Xerox Maintenance Management.* I will need two days to replan and talk to *Xerox Maintenance Management.*"

The first thing I said to the designer was, "Drop everything you're doing and work only on the *Seneca Falls* lathe concrete base drawings." He agreed.

The reason for this was, I needed drawings (2 weeks max), requiring a contractor to dig up the floor and place rebar (3 weeks+) then pour concrete with *Kinetic shocks* and cure (4weeks+).

When you add up the times, I have used 3 months+ and have no wiggle room.

I was determined to make this revised project a *"Go."*

During this time frame, I received a visit from Ramon. He was an engineer (with an unknown title) and I did not know to whom he reported. I tried to introduce myself, however, he appeared to be self-centered and have his own interests, without an introduction. Note, this was the same fellow who mistreated Fritz, (the Engineer assigned with me to the *Photoreceptor Division*) who in a sense forced Fritz to quit the company. As far as I was concerned, Ramon was an obstructionist, he would marginalize / undermine your work to gain power and overstep you at the first opportunity (this is also mentioned in Chapter XVI).

Ramon said to me, (after I resolved the massive diamond turning problem which had at times a production rate less than 10%), *"You would never be a model."* I looked him straight in the eye and said, *"I am not here to be a model, I am here as directed by the Vice President of Manufacturing Fabrication Engineering, to resolve your problems. Don't get in my way."* I could not have overstated the importance of my efforts any better. Yes, I fired the warning shot.

At this time, I decided to keep a *Rainy-Day* file about my accomplishments.

Part of the installation project for the diamond turning equipment was to test the *Seneca Falls Machine Company* lathe at their plant. The first test "<u>failed</u>" (Big Time) with marks on the photoreceptor at equally spaced intervals. I suspected a very large timing belt with a molded seam was the cause. The *Seneca Falls Machine Company* engineers worked all that evening and into the next morning. Mathematics proved the timing belt was the culprit. The timing belt was replaced with V-belts and the machine worked flawlessly.

The *Seneca Falls Machine Company* engineers could not believe the diamond finish the machine produced.

The *Seneca Falls Machine Company* lathe's initial cost to *Xerox* was \$250,000.^{00} and paid for itself, after 1000 photoreceptors were produced.

As a *Project Manager* in the *Photoreceptor Division*, I worked almost normal hours. My wife and son appreciated the extra time I spent with my family.

The *Project Timeline* <u>last</u> date was right on schedule, when the first special long photoreceptor was produced.

"Being straight forward and handling sensitive situations carefully is a very important role of being an engineer."

Donald A. Drexler

Photoreceptor Project Engineer
Photoreceptor Division
Xerox Corporation

Chapter XII - The Dolittle Mill

Once the special diamond turning equipment was completed, I was briefed of more responsibilities to be placed on my platter. Peter, my manager, as I mentioned earlier, was inspiring, very quiet and professional. We continued discreet conversations about sensitive situations, and I was always straight forward with him. Apparently, he liked bringing in the *Seneca Falls Machine Company Diamond Turning Equipment* three months early. This was a huge financial plus for *Xerox Corporation*.

My next endeavor would be to install the Dolittle Mill (the company name has been changed to protect the guilty). This mill would complete in one cycle (in the photoreceptor drum), the boring and chamfering of a hole for the *Automatic Document Control (ADC)* electronics. The chamfering tool (inside and outside) had to follow the curved surface of the photoreceptor drum. My initial thought was, I didn't think this was necessary and it could be completed totally with electronic sensors in the paper path. I was thinking too far ahead of myself.

I requested machine and tooling drawings, I had nothing, since everything was being designed and manufactured by the supplier Dolittle Tooling Company.

Three weeks later, I received the machine prints, and I recognized a major problem. The chamfering operation was performed in one operation, for the outside and inside of the photoreceptor drum. I was then advised it was too late for any revisions to the Dolittle Mill chamfering design.

I thought this concept was stupid at its best, especially with the tooling. I would have to live with it.

The mill was installed by the *Xerox Maintenance Department*. The tooling required a set-up, but we were without instructions from the Dolittle Tooling Company. Set-up Instructions were requested along with a second request, for tooling prints.

I was able to set the Dolittle mill up without proper instructions. This procedure was extremely complicated, and I suspected our *Amalgamated Clothing and Textile Workers Union* operator would have problems with setting up the tooling.

The Dolittle Tooling Company's Tooling Set-up Instructions finally arrived and required much additional input because of a lack of information. If that data had been issued to the *Xerox Production* floor, all the tooling would have been wrecked in one day. If I were to call the buyer and request a rewrite of the tool set up information, it would probably take weeks. I needed to get the Dolittle mill operational. I re-wrote and hand carried this to the *Xerox Photoreceptor Production* floor.

Many hours were spent with the *Amalgamated Clothing and Textile Workers Union* operator over the next almost three weeks making sure the operator understood a set-up error would destroy the tooling.

I requested the operator contact his supervisor and have him contact me when he had to change tooling because of wear. I expected the carbide tooling to last four to five weeks, because of a very light cut.

Just over two weeks later, I received a phone call that the tooling had to be replaced. As he changed the tooling, I walked him through each step very carefully, and explained the reason why. He appeared to understand what was required, I questioned him about the setting technique, and he responded reasonably well.

Just short of another three weeks later I stopped by the *Xerox Photoreceptor Production* floor at the Dolittle mill. The supervisor was there, and a maintenance worker was trying to set up the Dolittle mill.

I asked, "What was going on?" The response from the supervisor was, "Where were you last night at 8:30 pm?"

My response was, "Having supper with my wife in Niagara Falls, Canada." I also informed him, "I also stayed in Niagara Falls, New York, for the overnight and drove back to Rochester early this morning."

There were no further questions.

One of six tools (sent in with the Doolittle mill) was wrecked because of an improper set-up. I went over the set-up procedure with the union operator and the supervisor very thoroughly. This second diamond ground chamfering tool lasted almost three weeks. This was a much shorter tool life expectancy than I anticipated.

The next step was to take the two worn diamond ground chamfering tools along with the broken tool to the *Xerox Tool Room* in building 208 (Webster, New York). I still had not received tool drawings from the Dolittle Tooling Company. You might say, I had some choice words with the buyer.

The only way the *Xerox Tool Room* would be able to diamond regrind the two Dolittle tools, was to establish the primary and secondary reliefs on the tooling with a *Cincinnati Monoset* grinder. This required guess work on the part of the tool maker, which I was forced to accept, without a tooling print. The broken tool, I was informed, could not be salvaged.

I also knew each resharpening procedure would require five set-ups on a *Cincinnati Monoset* grinder. Special diamond wheels for both finish and rough grinding would be required. Each of the primary and secondary reliefs would require four grinding wheel changes. This would be time consuming, and finishing diamond grinding wheels would be extremely expensive.

Approximately five weeks lapsed, and the fifth tool was showing wear. I did not like the finish with the chamfering tool and decided to replace it to save life expectancy. I also needed to call the *Xerox Tool Room* manager and request a status on the two diamond ground chamfering tools they received for resurfacing.

The response was, "They were just about done, and you could pick them up the next morning."

The next morning, I hand carried the two diamond chamfering tools that required resurfacing to the *Xerox Tool Room* and picked up the two-diamond cutting tools which were just resurfaced. I also informed the *Tool Room Manager* that I expected to be back in about four weeks with more diamond resurfacing work.

Two weeks later while at home I received a call at 7:45 pm from the *Xerox Photoreceptor Production* supervisor and he stated he and the *Amalgamated Clothing and Textile Workers Union* operator could not set the diamond chamfering tool in the Dolittle mill.

I stated, "I would be there at 8:45 pm," my driving time from my home averaged about 50 minutes.

I followed my set-up instructions carefully and could not get the Dolittle Mill to perform. After checking all the settings, I could find nothing wrong. It was now after 11:00 pm and I was a little tired. I decided to use some tool makers bluing on the sides of the diamond ground chamfering tool. It worked and the *Xerox Tool Room* never resurfaced the secondary relief. The surface bluing showed a wear mark on the diamond tool secondary relief that prevented the tool from doing its job.

The next morning, I had two diamond chamfering tools that required secondary reliefs which would also require four-time consuming setups. It would have helped if I had a tool drawing with primary and secondary relief specifications. The buyer was going to hear about this <u>again.</u> The three diamond tools in the *Xerox Tool Room* for resharpening were "ready." However, in reviewing them, the secondary specification (relief) was never reground. <u>Suddenly</u>, I had zero tools available.

I needed to be calm, cool, and collected before I spoke to the *Xerox Tool Room* manager. I recognized this was a sensitive situation and I needed to be straight forward but not outspoken. I needed to reach out to the *Tool Room Manager*, because I believed the *Tool Maker* was not fulfilling performance criteria for his job position.

The *Xerox Tool Room* manager would bail me out and get the tools corrected. I explained what was required, and he obliged. However, the *Tool Maker*, with the *Amalgamated Clothing and Textile Workers Union,* severely reground the diamond surface which then lost considerable (70-80%) tooling life expectancy. His skills did not match the occupation requirement for this type of work. I knew the set-up procedure with a *Cincinnati Monoset* grinder would be a nightmare.

Two of the remaining five diamond chamfering tools now had a life expectancy of one resharpening regrind. I had expected resharpening lives to be somewhere between six to nine. There was no question the *Xerox Tool Maker* erred in the set-ups that caused shorter life expectancy.

A week later the *Xerox Tool Room* manager wrote a letter to me requesting this work be removed from the *Xerox Tool Room* in *Webster, New York.* I expected the *Amalgamated Clothing and Textile Workers Union* would have tried to stop this action. If the *Amalgamated Clothing and Textile Workers Union* knew I was involved, maybe that's why no action was ever to be taken.

A buyer was contacted to purchase additional tooling for the Dolittle Mill. We were close to a critical situation because of a lack of good tooling.

The <u>only</u> grinding machine that could grind or regrind the carbide tooling for the Dolittle Mill was a *Cincinnati Monoset Grinder*. This is a very complicated piece of equipment, and its cost was around 70 k. I heard estimates to make the special tools were between $ 1,650. to $ 2,000. Special diamond wheels would have cost (2) for finish grinds $1,800 each, and (2) rough grinds for $900 each. The special diamond wheels (most expensive) could easily be destroyed by one misstep by the *Tool Maker* because of the very bad tool design by the Dolittle Mill Company. My view from the design standpoint could be referred to as a GIGO (garbage in, garbage out).

I initially estimated we could get eight lives from each tool if the resharpening tool maker removed .004 to .005 inch per regrind. This could only be achieved if you had a skilled tool maker. That was a serious question that could not be answered.

This is what happens when you are left out or you are not given the opportunity for critical input with the initial design of specialized equipment.

The Dolittle Mill would eventually be turned over to the *Photoreceptor Process Engineers.*

I doubt any of the *Photoreceptor Engineers* had <u>any</u> knowledge required for the tool design process. This equipment should never have been purchased, especially regarding the tooling. That says very little for management planning. I suspect the *Process Engineers* if they planned input (especially with the tooling) for the Dolittle Mill without critical knowledge, then that would be detrimental and not beneficial.

I came to quickly understand the *Process Engineers* did not have the <u>required</u> engineering critical skills, and that was obvious with the loose diamonds. *Photoreceptor Management* also had a primary objective with the *Photoreceptor Lathe Department* to get them up and running, sometimes less than 10% productive, and the *Process Engineers* did not understand the diamond burnishing pressures involved. They did not have the critical skills that reasonable engineers understood.

However, they would do a good job at giving you the BS. Then *Photoreceptor Management* requested help from the *Manufacturing Fabrication Engineering Vice President*. That's when I was selected.

The Dolittle Mill sufficed until advanced electronic technology came about.

"Planning or thinking far ahead is acceptable, however, keep control of current activities."

Donald A. Drexler

Photoreceptor Project Engineer
Photoreceptor Division
Xerox Corporation

Donald A. Drexler

Chapter XIII - Installing a Still

After getting the *Photoreceptor Plant* production resolved because of the loose diamonds, then managing the installation of a special lathe to produce longer photoreceptors, then I went on to managing the installation of a special mill. Peter, my manager, now wants me to install a <u>still.</u>

The only thing I knew about a still, was an illegal moonshine operation in the city of *Rochester, NY* near *Manhattan Steet* back in the fifties. They were discovered by a painter who was working on a tall building and was getting tipsy from the exhaust fumes. They must have had a very high exhaust stack. According to the *Democrat & Chronicle*, if I recall, the *Fed's* raided the operation and stated the results were equivalent to *Schenley's or Seagram's*. The one thing that puzzled the *Fed's* was how they could get tractor trailers unloaded with large loads of sugar without being detected. Enough of that.

This equipment would be a *Branson Still* equivalent of *producing 90 gallons* per hour. That's equivalent to *2,160 gallons per day or 15,120 gallons per week*. This still would be used for reclaiming cleaning material for *Xerox* usage.

A plan would be put together under the direction of the manufacturer. This equipment would be enclosed and have an overflow sump only in case of emergency. As I recall, the sump never had one drop ever enter the sump (with new cleaning material or reclaimed material). My one concern was to get electricity installed and in talking with *Xerox Maintenance* that would not be a problem.

Testing of the by-product would be weekly by *Midland Chemical* and the still was performing extremely well without any problems. Testing was mandatory because the bi-product would draw moisture from the air and that would turn into hydrochloric acid which could result in a still shutdown. This happened in Building 208 (years before) when a cleaning station (its bottom ate itself up) by using the same biproduct (our current cleaning material), while everyone was on vacation. I could only refer to that as "Oops."

Then one day I received a phone call from the lobby front desk that the *Bureau of Alcohol, Tobacco, and Firearms (BATF)* federal people were here to see me.

My first reaction was because I was an *Executive Officer* with a sportsman's organization, we (the sportsman's organization) had a problem. All our organization's paperwork was always filed properly.

On entering the lobby there were two gentlemen. One was dressed in light blue trousers with a short sleeve light blue shirt and no tie, and the other in light tan trousers and a colorful short sleeve shirt and no tie. On introductions they showed me their credentials *(BATF)* and inquired about what I was doing with the still.

Their appearance immediately gave them away. They used me for a trip to *Rochester, New York*, so they could watch the *Ladies Professional Golf Association Tournament*.

The *Bureau of Alcohol, Tobacco, and Firearms* wanted to know what I was processing with the still.

I thought I would have some fun with these fellows.

My response was, "Well I did think about running *Apricot Brandy* through it."

With that response, I thought they were going to put me in hand cuffs.

I just politely mentioned, "Would you like to see the operation?"

They responded with a smile and said, "Yes, that's why we are here."

Why I Wasn't Fired at Xerox

I requested them to sign in at the *Xerox Lobby Desk* and mentioned I would show them the still and I would have them on the *Photoreceptor Production* floor for only a few minutes.

I requested them to be prepared if they were going to ask questions, so that they could talk with me in the lobby, after the session on the floor.

They appeared to be in a hurry, there were no questions, and they thanked me for the tour.

Postscript, "I never saw any paperwork."

"Whenever there are surprises, handle them professionally with care."

Donald A. Drexler

Photoreceptor Project Engineer
Photoreceptor Division
Xerox Corporation

Donald A. Drexler

Chapter XIV - Photoreceptor Fallout Costing

Hundreds of Thousands of Dollars

This may be one of the shorter chapters in this book; however, it will turn into a nightmare for an engineer, a manager, and *Production Control*. It would take a year to surface.

It had been only a month since my last annual review in the *Photoreceptor Division* and then my close friend Fritz decided to leave the company. Fritz stated to me, he remained determined and committed to the company but was exploited, verbally abused, and mistreated by one engineer. That same engineer was Ramon (in Chapter XI). On several occasions, I encouraged Fritz to be proactive, tactful, and good natured (these are the keys to effectiveness). Fritz felt he was not getting anywhere with Ramon, and Fritz's only satisfaction was to quit or retire from the company. This was a sad day for me.

Suddenly, everyone in the plant was called into a meeting. We were having photoreceptor problems in the coating process. It was contamination with an unknown cause. The problem was described in a forty-page report costing hundreds of thousands of dollars from Warren the *Photoreceptor Division Vice President*.

We were all advised to investigate this, and get it resolved. Some lots were 100% rejected, because of contamination. The tone and urgency were most noteworthy. My perseverance kept my sanity – knowing I was now working in someone else's territory… (damn the torpedo's). I recognized there are engineering boundaries and I would do everything to understand and tackle the problem, however, in the back of my mind, I also thought complicity might be involved. In a later chapter this would be proven. I would not hesitate to push for the good of the company. If there are challenges, I will push them without question, providing it is right for the corporation or the shareholders.

In researching the *Packaging / Handling Specifications* I found cardboard was specified to cover inside the cargo container. On checking *Plant Production* this was not being used. The bottom side of cargo containers were filthy. When one cargo container is set on top of another, the impact of setting it there would allow the filth on the bottom side to drop onto the photoreceptors in the lower cargo container.

I penned a letter to *Production Control, Photoreceptor Engineering and Management* to resolve the *Vice President's* forty-page letter regarding fall out with the photoreceptors, that cost hundreds of thousands of dollars.

My letter would be initially ignored. It might have been a deliberate cover-up. If this was deliberate it could not be discussed because I did not know who was involved.

A year later * when the *Vice President of the Photoreceptor Division* was finally informed of the Photoreceptor fallout situation directly by me, he was livid with rage. That rage was focused on all those who initially received my letter, which for one year, did not resolve the problem. There would be a shakeup.

* This happened because of one person in the *Xerox Photoreceptor Division* that was an obstructionist. He would marginalize or undermine your work to gain power for himself and overstep you at his first opportunity. I could never understand why one person would act this way. You might say I fired the first warning shot. This is well documented in Chapter XI.

(In Chapter XVI the fireworks will continue).

Having worked about one month as a *Photoreceptor Project Engineer*, I was advised the *5600 Copier / Duplicator Program* wanted me on board. I had no idea of what or how this may have happened. What happened is more than inspiring and this is well stated in Chapter XV.

"The keys to effectiveness are being proactive, tactful and being good natured."

Donald A. Drexler

Photoreceptor Project Engineer
Photoreceptor Division
Xerox Corporation

Donald A. Drexler

Chapter XV - A Cycle Switch With a Mind Of

Its Own

My first day arriving on site, I found over half of the *5600 Copier / Duplicator Production Engineers* knew of me from interactions with the *Fabrication Manufacturing Department*: in general, the welding department, organic and inorganic finishing, plastic injection, plasma spray, fabrication mills, drills, grinding and finishing. This included all the *Production Control Department*, and the *Manufacturing Engineering Standards Department.* All the *5600 Copier / Duplicator Production Engineers* were highly talented, diverse, and from all over the country. It was inspiring to be with them. The first week they were "*reaching out to me*" and "*welcoming me on board.*" Their ambition, leadership, and commitment, without question, was the "*Cream of the Crop*" at *Xerox.* This was better than a "Home coming."

The biggest surprise came next. George, my manager in the *Fabrication Welding Department,* was now working as a manager, with the *5600 Copier / Duplicator Production Management.* Now I knew how my name came up, while I was working in the *Photoreceptor Division.* George knew I never left a stone unturned, and this is well documented in Chapter VIII. That was when the *Xerox Amalgamated Clothing and Textile Workers Union (ACTWU)* didn't have a chance against my well-thought-out plan and common sense for a union behavioral problem.

My first assignment by George was to resolve a *Production Timing Rate*, which you might say was out of control and unresolved.

The two production ladies, Roberta, and Roxanne could not meet the *Production Rate* of twenty-nine minutes with cycle switch settings. At times they would spend three and one-half hours to complete one unit. They decided to take this problem to the *5090 Copier / Duplicator Management, Sunrise Meeting.* This was open to all *Amalgamated Clothing and Textile Workers Union (ACTWU)* workers who had issues or problems within the corporation.

The two ladies stated they could not make or meet the production rate and they were frustrated. The foreman was unable to help. The *Time Study Department* had overwhelming and compelling data that sixteen settings could be made and there would be no revisions with the *Time Study*. It was easy to recognize without debate, this now was a *Management Problem.*

My *Manager* George and Fred the *Area Manager* approached me to investigate the cycle switch operation, because a lot of people were involved, and everything was on the table. My first statement was, I needed to visually review the procedures in place on the production floor. I spent most of the day with the union ladies, avoiding any negative conversations, along with extensive precautions because of *Union Rules*. I could not put my hands on union work... and this was looking more and more like a crisis. There was no end in sight.

The next day in the lab I spent checking the micro switches with a sophisticated set-up for variances with activation. My expectation was focused on defective switches. However, the micro switches adhered to specifications far better with repeatability at the activation point. My next step was to investigate the cams for any revisions. No revisions could be verified with design or procurement. The mold for the cams could undergo clean-up, however without a deviation, if maintaining specifications. I was failing to uncover the problem. I still suspected the cams were the problem.

Why I Wasn't Fired at Xerox

I needed a "Head-to-Head" match-up with *Xerox Management*. Meeting with my *manager* George and Fred the *Area Manager*, I requested hands on with the cycle switch procedure. I would now be taking work away from the *Union*. They went to the *union (ACTWU)* and came back stating, "You can't do that." My response to them was, "Then, I cannot help you, you need to get someone else involved." I needed to make that statement as a Game Changer, because this was another Pandora's Box, I always had a standing invitation to get along well with everyone. The *Union* was not cooperating.

My *Manager* and the *Area Manager* went back to the *Union* and the *Union* stated, "You could sit down at the bench, with hands on, when no union workers were around." That meant well after 11:00 pm. This would be another long night. My instincts changed with a different approach along with my enthusiasm and expectations. My *manager* George knew I at times would use unorthodox approaches to take advantage of opportunity.

Now above all, I always strived for a better workplace, and I also believed any barrier could be broken. It was evident with this situation I needed to maintain unity with the union workers. I also needed to reach out to the ladies and focus on fitting in without division. This was a "once-in-a-lifetime opportunity."

At 11:30 pm that night with no one around, I attempted to set the sixteen cycle switch settings on one unit. After one and a half hours I had no solution to the problem, and I needed to take a different direction.

It was now after 1:00 am in the morning when I decided to remove a perfectly working cycle switch from one of the machines on the line. This was done to find out what the settings were. If I got caught at this, someone would want me fired. It took me forty minutes to disassemble the unit from the machine. Not having the right tools didn't help.

The next step was to put this unit in the preset fixture and very carefully record the settings. I also marked the settings with a number 2 pencil over the setting lights on the gray painted setting fixture. These were barely visible. To say anything the settings were all over the place. The variance was fifteen minutes to three and ½ hours. (Example of settings were: fifteen minutes equaled one quarter turn and one hour equaled one complete turn of the screw that engaged the micro switch). I set three units at the computer table; these were identified to be tested by *Union* personnel. I expected to have a *union* person ask me that morning who preset the three units? The disassembled unit was replaced in line after a second test confirmed an acceptable assembly. Additional time was taken to replace the unit, making sure quality came first. While doing all this my anxiety was high expecting a *union* person would reprimand me for taking *union* work away from a *union production worker*. Well after all the *Union* did say, "I could do this when no one was around."

At 2:30 am that morning, I was replacing the borrowed tooling, tidying up the area and hoping I would be home to get some rest by 3:30 am that morning. My drive to work was about forty-five minutes.

The next day, I overslept. I woke up at 9:40 am, had a quick shave, some orange juice, and a cookie for breakfast. I arrived at work, late-morning and the union workers were cleaning up for the lunch break at 11:00 am.

I stopped by to say Good Morning to Roberta, one of the *union* ladies, and mentioned the switches could now be set. Her response was "No Way." I then said, "We need an agreement with you and Roxanne, and I will be back after lunch." Later Roberta and Roxanne were waiting for me, and I mentioned again that the switches could be set. Roberta interrupted and grabbed a cycle switch and said, "You're so damn smart, let me see you set it" and handed me an unset cycle switch unit to set. I accepted it with a smile and sat down at the preset fixture. I noticed my number 2 pencil markings <u>were</u> <u>just</u> <u>visible</u> above the setting lights. After about four minutes I handed Roberta the cycle switch and said this is set. She immediately took it to the computer and the results were "Accept." Her response was, "Dumb Luck, you can't do it again." My response was, "Yes I can." She immediately grabbed another unit and handed it to me and said, "Let me see you do it again." After about four minutes, I handed her the second unit. She immediately put it in the computer and the result was "Accept." She then said, "What are you doing?" My response was "<u>I</u> <u>need</u> <u>to</u> <u>have</u> <u>an</u> <u>agreement</u> <u>with</u> <u>both</u> <u>of</u> <u>you</u>." They agreed. I stated, "If anyone comes into the area and inquires, "What are you doing? You tell them you are following the process. Do not tell them the *Xerox Process* or *Don Drexler's Process*, just say you are following the process." I suspected if *Time Study* got involved with this, they would cut the rate so it could not be attained. Also, the *Xerox Time Study Department* stated, "They would not change the rate." I have seen this on many an occasion where the *Company* and *Union* would go in different directions. All I wanted to do was unite myself with these two ladies.

After two days of production, they had two additional days of production ahead of the line and they were socializing with their friends at the other end of the plant. Each time that I was in the area, they would invite me in for coffee. Eventually, I was allowed to carry fixtures and products to any place in the plant without being written-up. The two ladies told me one day, they said to their union, "If *Don Drexler* wants to do something, let him do it." I did not anticipate that.

About three weeks later, the girls had about seven racks (more than a week's supply) of cycle switches ahead of the line, this was somewhat of a distraction. Gary, the *supervisor* on the floor said nothing. I realized and expected to hear about this any day. This could turn into quite a predicament but protecting everyone's image would come first.

Five months later, on arriving at work, my *Manager* and the *Area Manager* were at the entrance to my office. One had his arm up on the door jam and the other had his arm also up on the opposite door jam. This was so I could not enter my office. My *manager* said, "What did you do on the *Production Floor*?" My response was, "I don't know what you are talking about?" His response was, "the *Cycle Switch*." I then said, "They are following the process." Then both said in unison, "Yea, we heard that last night." I could never have come up with a more brilliant plan.

As I said in my *Philosophy; Communication* is very important, that is what *Xerox Corporation's Philosophy* has always been; Create a vision and get others to accept and embrace it, paving the way with favorable results.

- -

The following footnote has very little to do with my position at *Xerox Corporation*, but it indirectly ties into my goals, determination, and performance with the company. In *1977* our *New York State Governor Hugh Carey* stated he would support at the highest level *The Empire State Games* for all sports. I thought this would be an excellent opportunity to develop into a top competitor. Rifle competition would be my sport. My involvement would help promote the competition and its image.

I would need to focus on two goals. 1) The equipment would require extensive and intensive testing which would result, eventually, in significant score improvement. 2) I realized my mental and physical properties needed to be addressed for endurance. All of this would not be easy, but I was determined.

At the *Opening Ceremony at the Empire State Games 1978*, a very small young girl (say 14 years old from *Buffalo,*

New York) behind me, touched my arm and said, "Are you a coach or a competitor?" My response to that was, "I am a competitor." She then said, "Whatever you do, you must be very good at it." I was past my prime (at 43 years of age) and what the young girl said to me, I will always remember. That young lady took a medal at the *Empire State Games* in *1978* on the balance beam.

I was up against the top competitors in *New York State*. All the competitors were *Sectional* or *Regional* Winners, and many were *National Record holders*. My objective and goals paid off. I took the *Gold Medal* at the *Empire State Games*. The following year *1979*, was a repeat with another *Gold Medal*.

I was amazed, the *Xerox World Magazine* printed an excellent article about my accomplishment with the *Empire State Games*. My philosophy and determination at work or at play would never waver.

"Opportunities enable you to achieve your dreams."

Donald A. Drexler

Senior Engineer
5600 Mid Volume Copier / Duplicator
Xerox Corporation

Donald A. Drexler

Chapter XVI - A Review That Would Blow Up

This Chapter is a continuation from Chapter XIV when you were warned about fireworks.

Having worked in the *Xerox 5600 Copier / Duplicator* area for 11 months, I finally received a review from the *Photoreceptor Division* for one month, (the first month) in a twelve-month cycle.

The review was processed by Burt, a new manager of the *Photoreceptor Division* of whom I had very little correspondence. In reading the review I was shocked. It was not accurate. It was deceiving, misrepresenting and untruthful. This review was nothing more than Character Assassination.

If you read Chapter XIV, on photoreceptor fallout, costing hundreds of thousands of dollars, you discovered that one engineer (Ramon) was maneuvering for power, and only playing by his rules. Fritz the other engineer (whom I worked with from the *Manufacturing Fabrication Engineering Section*) was also directed by the *Vice President of Manufacturing Fabrication Engineering* to resolve the problems in the *Photoreceptor Division.* Of course, we were outsiders, no question about that…Damn the torpedoes. I knew from day one, I would need to keep a rainy-day file (for a future time of need).

In studying the review, which I was not given an opportunity for input, it was obvious to see there was deliberate deception and vengeance. Someone was retaliating to get satisfaction. Possibly this was because of a statement Ramon made to me in Chapter XIV, *"You will never be a model."* Then I looked him straight in the eye and said, *"I am not here to be a model, I am here as directed by the Vice President of Manufacturing Fabrication Engineering, to resolve your problems, don't get in my way."* I could not have overstated the importance of my efforts any better. For him to attempt or restrict my path forward, was not something I would allow or stand for.

The review had a rating of two on it. With a two on the review, I felt I would be on the curb stone the next day. I was not about to allow this in my review because it contained lies about me.

I put together a seventeen-page rebuttal with the review. This included my manager's weekly and monthly reports (that stated just the opposite of what was in the current review) with my status reports. One item in the review stated, "I missed a machine installation date." When in fact, I brought in the equipment three months earlier at the request of the buyer.

This is a summary of what happened. Our *Xerox Procurement buyer* stated, "A buyer with *International Harvester* cancelled an order ahead of our machinery to be built by *Seneca Falls Machine Company (S.F.M.C.)."* Our *Xerox* buyer then requested, "Could *S.F.M.C.* bring our order in three months ahead of time?" Hearing that I knew my schedule was going to change drastically. I stated, "I could not answer that until, I could redo my *Xerox Installation Timeline* and discuss this with *Xerox Maintenance Management* who were responsible for electrical and mechanical installation." I was responsible for the design and installation of the entire project including the concrete base and the *Kinetic shocks* for control of the diamond finish for the photoreceptors. The concrete curing was one month, which just fit in the newly revised *Timeline.* Two days later, I had a *"Go"* for installation of the equipment, with the three-month early placement. I knew I would be working long hours.

Another item in my rebuttal was, I penned a letter to resolve a "major problem" with *Photoreceptor* fallout. This letter was sent to *Production Control, Photoreceptor Engineering and Management* with resolution to our *Photoreceptor Vice President's* forty-page letter, regarding fall out, that cost hundreds of thousands of dollars. Reference to the *Photoreceptor Vice President's* forty-page letter was never mentioned in my manager's review. To leave this out, I suspect it was intentional. My letter clearly stated the *Photoreceptor Plant Engineering and Production Control* <u>were</u> <u>not</u> <u>following</u> *Xerox Packaging / Handling Specifications* which were clearly spelled out.

In researching the *Xerox Packaging / Handling Specifications* I found cardboard was not specified in the production process or used to cover the cargo container.

A lot of thoughts crossed my mind, was this done deliberately? If that was the case, then *Production Control* should have corrected this on day one. If there was a suggestion submitted by a *Xerox* person, the *Xerox Photoreceptor Engineer* should have rejected it immediately. I also suspect *Xerox Management* was never told about this and there was a cover-up.

The next day (a year after the VP's 40-page report), I decided to visit the *Xerox Photoreceptor Division, Production Plant* and check to see if they were using cardboard specifically on the cargo container top.

On checking the *Xerox Photoreceptor Division Production Plant,* cardboard was not being used to protect the photoreceptors. Then, why was *Production Control* and the *Photoreceptor Plant Engineering* not using *Xerox Packaging / Handling Specifications?* At the same time, I was given handwritten copies of my review that was written by (guess who) Ramon and not by my new *Photoreceptor Manager.* This was now, clearly, a case of retaliation to get satisfaction with Ramon. Apparently, this fellow favored personal gain for someone else's destruction.

I requested a review with the *Photoreceptor Engineering Manager,* and he stated, "I will not change the review." I mentioned "I would take it to the next level." I was unable to have a review with the *Photoreceptor Area Manager.*

The next day with the seventeen-page review rebuttal, in hand, along with a copy of my letter regarding resolution with the *Vice President's* forty-page *Photoreceptor Problem,* I decided to head for the *Photoreceptor Vice President's Office* at 5:45 pm.

Warren the *Photoreceptor Vice President* was not in, however his secretary welcomed me. I mentioned I penned a letter about the *Vice President's* forty-page *Photoreceptor Problem* and handed her a copy, she reviewed it and suddenly said, "Are you the author of this letter? My response was, "Yes."

She immediately said, "Warren the *Photoreceptor Vice President* is going to want to talk to you." I immediately picked up on her reactions that were urgent and pressing.

On arriving home (about a 45-minute trip) my wife greeted me at the door and said, someone by the name of Warren called and he will call back at 7:00 pm.

At 7:00 pm the phone rang, and I was talking to Warren. He wanted to know if I could be in his office at 7:00 am. I said, "yes." There was a long pause, and then he said, "I have a staff meeting at 7:00 am." The next thing he said, "I'm cancelling my staff meeting. I want you in my office at 7:00 am." I mentioned, "I will be there."

The next morning the meeting was very cordial. His first question was, "How come I am finding out about this a year later?" I told him that I wrote a response almost a year ago to his 40-page report. My response went to his *Photoreceptor* people and was apparently not passed up in the chain of command. Now I was receiving a bad review for that first month of a twelve-month cycle which contained a 2 rating. I felt I would be on the curb stone the next day. I mentioned the review was misrepresenting and misleading for my work, let alone being dishonest and deceitful. I handed him my seventeen-page rebuttal, that well documented what happened with my manager's weekly and monthly reports.

I also said to him, "If my review would not be changed, I felt I would be on the curbstone the next morning. If that should happen, I would be on a plane that same day and I would be at *Xerox Headquarters, Stamford, Connecticut* talking to *CEO, C. Peter McCollough*" and let him know what is happening in the *Webster Photoreceptor Division.*

Warren said, "You will not have to do that" and then said, "I have a problem at my end, that I need to address."

I left with a smile and a comfortable feeling.

Returning to the *Xerox 5600 Copier / Duplicator,* I was approached by Fred the *Area Manager* late that morning. Fred asked, "Do you have a problem here?" My response was, "Here no, but for one year ago, in the *Photoreceptor Division*, yes."

Fred then said, "Come on down to my office and let's talk." I grabbed a copy of the seventeen-page rebuttal.

In his office Fred was reviewing the seventeen-page rebuttal and shaking his head side to side. Fred could not believe what was said and stated, "How can someone contrive this!" He realized this review was misrepresenting and misleading my activities. I then directed his attention to the *Photoreceptor Vice President's* forty-page letter, regarding fall out, that cost hundreds of thousands of dollars. A year ago, I wrote a corrective action letter to *Production Control, Photoreceptor Engineering and Management.* No action was taken and the high cost of rejected photoreceptors continued. In the back of my mind, I only had one question, Was the photoreceptor contamination continued deliberately to create overtime?

At that point Fred's phone rang, and then he said to the caller, "Why are you talking to me, why don't you talk to him, here he is!" Fred handed me the phone and I said, "Good morning." I was now talking to David, the *Photoreceptor Plant Manager.* Suddenly my review was being revised!

The next morning, I picked up my revised review from the *Photoreceptor Area Manager.* I asked one question to the *Photoreceptor Area Manager.* "How come my review was revised from a two, to a perfect score?" I never received an answer, but I did get a side-to-side head shake. It was obvious by his reactions that he needed to investigate what was going on, especially with *the 40-Page Fallout Report* from the *Photoreceptor Vice President.*

The next day I shared the revised review with my *Mid Volume Manager.* After a few minutes he paused and mentioned, "Why should something like this happen?"

I did not want to make a statement; however, I did say, "There were problems in the *Photoreceptor Plant* that needed attention."

I won't go into detail, but some people just kind of "dropped out of sight."

"When you are faced with Complex Problems there is Great Wisdom in being strong-willed and forthright with a positive approach."

Donald A. Drexler

Senior Engineer
5090 Mid Volume Copier / Duplicator
Project Manager ~ Photoreceptor Division
Xerox Corporation

Chapter XVII - A Bearing That Stopped

Everything

The *5600 Mid Volume Copier / Duplicator* used three Hellfury lateral bearings in the optics. The optics traversed across two precision shafts to scan the document. The optics lens assembly was my responsibility.

Suddenly, we are having problems in the *Final Run and Test*. I suspected the bearing/housing was the problem source because jams were the major problem. I pulled prints for the bearing assembly and the only thing that *Receiving Inspection* could verify or inspect was the outside diameter, inside diameter and the overall length. All the dimensions were within specification. The lowest grade for a bearing would be Class 1. This bearing did not have a classification. *Receiving Inspection* would not perform a purge of the system because everything met specification. Therefore, I have a functional problem. The next step was to contact the buyer and have *Supplier Quality Assurance* investigate the bearing problem. The bearing problem was getting worse in the *Final Run and Test*. Another well-known bearing manufacturer in the *United States* produced excellent bearings, however our supply was very limited, and these bearings worked extremely well. I tried to expedite an order for these better bearings and was told they had a long lead time. It almost seemed there was a divergent or deliberate plan being played and I was the problem, not the bearings. I was straight forward and emphasized we had a serious problem, and this could lead to shutting down production. I also researched *Dunn and Brad Street* to make sure Hellfury (the bearing supplier) was not owned by a competitor or even aligned with a business rival. They were not.

A few days later mid-morning Wednesday another manager Harley, whom I worked with very well, came to me and said, "Hellfury wanted 300 bearings tested in line, with *Final Run and Test*." Now, I suspected the *Xerox* buyer was (going around me) using my *5600 Mid Volume Management*, as a tool against me, because the buyer would not believe there was a problem. To test 300 bearings would mean special paperwork would be required to track the three bearings in each copier. Time required in minor subs, then major subs would take about 5 to 7 days, line assembly 10 to 14 days, then *Final Run and Test* another 10 to 14 days. Therefore, we are talking at least one month plus for testing without interruptions.

I said to Harley, "I am not testing these bearings; however, I plan to stay here all night to undertake an intensive review and find out what is wrong with these bearings." I also mentioned, "I needed to go up to town, to the toy store and buy a pound of *Playdough.*" He looked at me and said, "Whatever you need." I wanted the *Playdough* because the *Assembly Production* ladies on the floor mentioned there were extraneous ball bearings that they would find, then throw them away. I mentioned to the *Assembly Production* ladies, that if they found any additional bearings I needed to know immediately. I wanted the *Playdough* to place around my desk surface to capture any loose ball bearings. At the same time the *Final Run and Test* workers mentioned the problem escalated and it was border line to out of control. I called my wife and mentioned I did not know how long I would be working, but expected to be home by 9:30 pm, so do not make dinner for me.

5:00 pm. Wednesday my desk surface was bordered with *Playdough,* and it was intended to capture loose ball bearings, and I did not want to be disrupted. Out of the one hundred bearings, I started to mark the housings 1 through 100. I marked sixty-five and in the process a ball bearing was loose on my desk surface. I stopped marking the metal housings at the sixty-five count. Reviewing the races, I found the housing that the ball came out of. My first reaction was that the ball (size .0625") could not have got out of the race. I went to pick the ball up and in touching it moved, clump, clump (clump is slang for movement-stop-movement-stop). The ball had a massive cavity on its surface. This was Exhibit #1.

I then placed a bearing/housing (a lateral bearing) on a precision optics shaft and moved it up and down on the shaft, while biasing the bearings at various rotational locations during the test. Of the sixty-five housings I could detect sensitive/unusual movement in thirty-three of the housings. This was just over 50% of my initial sample. I suspected there would be implications.

9:30 pm Wednesday, again I called my wife and mentioned with an apology that it would be early morning before I would be able to leave work and if she needed me, to call my *Xerox* work phone. I was Blessed to have my wife understand the situation and she stated my work would always come first. She cared and was always at my side. I could have never found a better wife, thank you dear Lord.

Next step was to obtain sample bottles from the *Xerox Metrology Lab.*, as I needed to keep everything separated. With no one in the *Xerox Metrology Lab.*, I lost over one hour trying to locate small sample bottles. Obtained five bottles with screw on lids.

My next step was to remove one of the retainer rings from each housing and visually inspect everything. The evidence was overwhelming. At this point I went back to the *Xerox Metrology Lab* for another twenty sample bottles. I found more than 50% of the metal housings had deep internal heat-treating cracks. However, there was no evidence of a crack on the outside of the housing, and it appeared the manufacturer was roll-burnishing (outer skin) the housing to hide or cover the crack. An acid test proved some cracks were very deep and it would bleed through. Metal chips were found in the housing with the bearings and unknown foreign material. One housing was broached on an angle, while finish grinding it would not clean up on each opposing end sides. I suspect the housing when broached had metal chips under one side, at the base. The finish grind had a finish of more than 60 ^{rms} (Root Mean Square), this is a <u>very</u> <u>poor</u> <u>finish</u> for use with a precision bearing.

This evidence was overwhelming and beyond debate. All of this was pointing to an "Out of Control" process. I realized the implications could be mind boggling and the worst chilling effect would be a production shut down.

> *First,* I needed a deliberate plan, and I would need to focus on a production goal.

> *Second*, my primary objective would be shipping machines.

> *Third,* I would need to force my hand by creating (you might say) an ice breaker effect, requiring upper management approval. My strategy to a path forward would be simple but unconventional. Hang on.

Thursday 3:30 am, I left work after a very long fatigued day. Drove around *Webster, New York*, looking for an open restaurant, found everything was closed. Drove into *Rochester* and found a diner open and parked directly in front. One person was at the counter and a cook. The cook requested what I would like, and my response was something light. The person at the counter said, "*Get the Garbage Plate.*" Not knowing what it was, I decided to order it, because it was recommended. The plate consisted of a hotdog, hamburger, beans, and potato. Well, it was loaded with extra *Cayenne Pepper*. I couldn't finish it and drank a lot of coffee and water. On getting into my car, I realized my clothing stunk of *Cayenne Pepper*. It was a cold day and I drove home with the car windows wide open. Hung my clothing in the garage, took a shower and drank some Listerine. I climbed into bed without waking the wife and set the alarm clock for 6:30 am. It was now 5:30 am. Well, I didn't get much sleep and the next thing I knew the alarm clock went off. Shutting the alarm off, I laid back and when I woke up it was 10:20 am. A quick shave, some orange juice and a cookie was all I had time for. My wife understood my commitment and I thank *God* every day, for her love and support.

Thursday 11:15 am. Arrived at work. Immediately I called Martin the *Senior Designer* and stated we had a flaw in the design criteria and if I could not get good bearings, I would have to shut the *Assembly Production Line* down. He said, "What?" I said, "You heard me." He was in my office within fifteen minutes. At that point, I was still physically drained and explaining the avalanche of data, which was devastating, he was immediately convinced to confront the problem head on. I mentioned the Hellfury bearing did not have an *American Bearing Manufactures Association (ABMA)* class category which allows the *Annular Bearing Engineers Committee (ABEC)* to assign a class number. There are five classes 1, 3, 5, 7 and 9. The *ABEC 9* is a higher class with higher precision specifications. We should have had at least an *ABEC 1*, there was no classification.

His approach would be to take photographs with a microscope (blown up images) and have copies to me the next day, Friday morning. He would take everything and dissect the material for the purpose of microscope photographing. I said to him, "Whatever you need to do, is fine with me, but don't lose anything." He also would go to his *Vice President* and get a "*Hold Work Order*" which would require the *Vice President's* signature, this was being placed against Hellfury. No activity (purchasing) with Hellfury could be done until this problem is resolved.

That afternoon I met with Fred the *Area Assembly Manager* of the *5600 Mid Volume Copier / Duplicator* and mentioned, "More than likely I would have to *Shut Assembly Production* down." With that said, I must say, I captured his attention immediately. I was very candid with my analysis and explained the consequences with patience and perseverance.

My plan was to *"Leap Frog"* the known good bearings we had in *Final Run and Test* and then ship the machines to the warehouse <u>without</u> <u>bearings</u>. Because of this purge the buyer would have to be engaged to correct the dilemma. I also advised the *Area Production Manager* that compromise is not in my dictionary. We would "maintain the strategy" that we would shut *Assembly Production* down, if we could not get acceptable bearings. The *Area Assembly Production Manager* supported and acknowledged my approach with assertiveness, because there was "nowhere else to go."

Friday 10:15 am. The *Senior Designer* came into my office with a smile and said, "Good Morning" handing me a huge package of 4x6 photographs of the bearing problems. I returned the salutation with a welcome and a gesture for coffee. He mentioned his *Vice President* had signed a *Hold Work Order (HWO)* against Hellfury, on that, the feeling that overcame me I could never express. Once a *HWO is signed by a VP, we cannot do business with that company until the HWO is resolved.* I thanked the *Senior Designer.*

Of all the photographs, I selected twelve, the cream of the crop. I started to put the photographs on individual sheets of paper, identifying each exhibit (A, B, C, etc.) with each problem clearly stated. I would have twelve Exhibits.

Suddenly Harley, one of our excellent *Managers* with the *5600 Mid Volume Copier / Duplicator,* came into my office and said, "I was wanted in the *Auditorium* with *Xerox Procurement* at 1:00 pm today." I said, "What's this about?" His response was, "I don't know." My first reaction was, he is an excellent manager, "He is not telling me something." OK, I thought to myself, now I am navigating and damming the torpedoes. I would counter this with, "Harley, I would like to buy your lunch today and have you go with me to the *Auditorium. "* His response was, "You can handle it." I suspect this is about the Hellfury bearing crisis.

Why I Wasn't Fired at Xerox

Friday 11:00 am, I am panicking to complete twelve sets of the various exhibits. Consequently, each package would have twelve different (problems) copies stapled together, totaling one hundred and forty-four copies. Checked the time and now the *Xerox Cafeteria* is closed. Placed the twelve packages in my brief case and headed for a restaurant in Webster, New York. With little time, I had a fish sandwich and a happy ending. Immediately left for the *Xerox Auditorium in Procurement*.

Friday 1:07 pm, I entered the *Xerox Auditorium in Procurement* and took a quick head count of twenty-seven people waiting for me. The only place for me to sit down was directly across from the buyer. There were no introductions. I got the feeling this was like the Spanish Inquisition, with infamously brutal methods. People at the meeting were from *Xerox Supplier Quality Assurance,* Hellfury the supplier - *Officers and Quality Control, Xerox Receiving Inspection and Xerox Management with Procurement.* I suspected this was nothing more than a setup to get me fired.

Without introductions, the meeting started out with *Xerox Supplier Quality Assurance* testifying this was the best company they ever worked with, and they earned all kinds of awards. I listened to this for about thirty minutes. At the same time, I am getting an evident sense, the buyer is skillfully setting me up for a power grab to show, he is more knowledgeable about this company than I. It was obvious they were painting a picture of a company that was honest and true by winning awards. I was reluctant to believe this, but I thought it was at least entertaining. I was determined to say nothing until I was spoke to.

Finally, the buyer said to me, "Do you have anything to say?"

My response was, "I will not install a Hellfury bearing in our product. If I cannot obtain quality bearings, I will shut the *Xerox 5600 Mid Volume Copier / Duplicator, Production Line* down.

The buyer then said, "You do not have the authority to shut the *Production Line* down and you do not have proof."

My response was, "I have already issued instructions and have taken steps with the *Area Manager of the Production Line.*"

The buyer again said, "You don't have the proof."

My response to that was, "You know me, I worked for you for almost five years in the *Manufacturing Fabrication Engineering Department* and I received from you the best merit increases. I basically maxed out in pay grade and was offered a position from another manager which I accepted. You know I never left a stone unturned."

The buyer again said, "You don't have the proof."

My response to that was, "You should have made a phone call to me, I could have stopped this meeting."

The buyer again said, "You still don't have the proof."

My response to that was, "You provided me with three hundred bearings to be tested in the *5600 Mid Volume Copier / Duplicator,* that would take me well over a month, possibly closer to two months. I received those bearings on Wednesday. I hope you don't expect the testing to be complete in two and a half days. Besides I will not even think about testing them in the *5600 Mid Volume Production Line.*

The buyer again said, "You still don't have the proof."

Saying this five times, I triggered him to raise his voice but, I wanted to ignore that. I stood up, opened my briefcase, and took out the twelve stapled bearing problems with photographs for each Exhibit. Then stated, "I counted twenty-seven people here, I'm sorry but I only have twelve copies well documenting the Exhibits with the Hellfury bearing problem…I have more important problems to care for." ... Then walked out the door.

I returned to my office and let the *5600 Engineering Management* know in a positive and sensitive way what transpired.

Just a note: Very seldom is their instant success with a problem, it takes strategy, determination, endurance, and commitment with the right people. If I had to add one more it would be leverage.

About three weeks later Harley, one of the *5600 Engineering Managers* came to me and needed some hardware. On a slip was some hardware that the production workers pick up with a magnet and scrap each day. I mentioned, "We have a scrap box on the production floor where I could get the hardware after work." Harley said, "No, I would like you to get it from a certain hardware store on *Penfield Road* and bring back a receipt." I said, "No problem." I went straight to the hardware department, and I was shocked at what I saw, the bearing buyer was working for the hardware store.

Two months later, I was talking to Martin the *Senior Designer* about the bearings we were using from another US Manufacturer and that they were working flawlessly. I also mentioned, "I had no update about the Hellfury problem." The *Senior Designer* stated, "A very large quantity of Hellfury bearings were <u>purchased</u> against the *Vice President's Hold Work Order*." Hearing that, I was not about to second guess what happened, I will let the reader connect the dots.

Donald A. Drexler

"If your wife or significant other appreciates and understands your commitment with work, then, Thank God every day for her love and support."

Donald A. Drexler

Senior Engineer
5600 Mid Volume Copier / Duplicator
Xerox Corporation

Chapter XVIII - The Coffee Pot That Beat the

System

History: In building 208R the employees had a "honor system" coffee station. The employees would donate small change which covered the costs of all the supplies. To obtain water for the two 20 cup coffee makers, the engineers had to modify a gallon milk carton by cutting a hole about ¾ up on one side of the jug. Therefor you could only fill the jug with about 3 quarts from the bathroom sink. I was very sensitive about the hygiene of obtaining water from the bathroom and did not like it. We were making five trips (about 140 feet round trip) to the bathroom with two jugs daily. The coffee pot was in an area that had water lines directly overhead at the ceiling.

I decided to propose a *Maintenance Work Order* to install a water drop with a shut off. My colleagues supported this 100%. The *Maintenance Work Order* was presented to George, one of our managers, with a productivity loss time 50 minutes per day (because of the back-and-forth trips to the distant bathroom). The lost time calculated by engineering was estimated at $5,200.^{00} per year. The *Maintenance Work Order* was denied because maintenance wanted $3,000.^{oo}. Of course, this would have to be scoped out, material ordered, and installed. We would be lucky to have it in three months or more.

A few days later, I was motivated to take this front and center, I had a brilliant plan, <u>without</u> <u>management</u> <u>approval,</u> but I needed "opportunity and timing." Also, I was not about to share this with anyone in the immediate timeframe.

I just happened to be on the production floor about a week later with an *Electrical Engineer* by the name of Larry when suddenly the opportunity was about to strike. I said to Larry "Don't say a word." On approaching two contractors well into their retirement, I noticed they were having coffee from thermos bottles with makeshift chairs and a table. With a smile I said, "Good Morning" and they responded also with a smile and a cordial "Good Morning." Then I asked, "what are you working on?" Their response was "Everything, electrical, plumbing and air." I then said, "Sounds like you are going to be here a long time!" Their response was "Six to nine months." I then said, "How would you like all the free coffee you can drink every day and donuts every Friday morning." That got their attention. Their response was "What do you need?" My response was, "A water drop the other side of the wall behind you." After showing them the area and the coffee pots their response was, "We should be able to handle that."

Less than ten minutes later, Larry came into my office and said, "Don, you've got to see this." Larry took me over to the coffee area and there was a brand new ¾" copper water line totally installed and flushed out. The line had a 90-degree shut off and a flexible line to fill each coffee pot. Larry looked at me, shook his head side to side with a smile I will never forget. This was a no brainer.

Mission Accomplished.

A week later while I was getting a cup of coffee, George my *manager* came in also to get a cup of coffee. While getting his coffee he noticed the newly installed water line. Suddenly, he said to me, "Who put this in?" My response to him was, "I thought you signed the *Maintenance Work Order*." His response was, "No way would I sign that" (because of the expensive maintenance cost). When George never saw an expense for this, he forgot all about it but suspected I had something to do with it.

All I can say is, "Suspecting is one thing, doing is totally different."

George, the manager who rejected the work order to install the water line for the coffee pot, retired a year later. That day, he came to me, and stated, "He was going to take me to dinner that evening." My response was, "I was extremely busy with problems and my wife doesn't know about this." His response was he had already called my wife. After dinner that evening, he wanted to know, *"how I pulled off the above,"* which benefited everyone, including the contractors. He could not believe how I accomplished this in just a few minutes. I will never forget his smile that evening.

In researching my files, I found a copy of the small sign I had made up that was on the wall, just over the coffee pots and I thought I would show it here.

This coffee pot has
no set price.
Whatever you feel it's
worth is acceptable.
Please… just keep the
area clean & the water
at a respectable level
Thank you

Many engineers and managers asked me, "How did you do this?" My response was always, "Whenever a person contributes, success follows."

Final thought.

> *"We are always transformed when we learn through our differences.*
>
> *If there are engineering boundaries, I will push them. If there are challenges, I will meet them head on... I am also here to inspire."*

Donald A. Drexler

Senior Engineer
5090 Mid Volume Copier / Duplicator
Xerox Corporation

Chapter XIX - Installing a Master Computer

For Testing The 5090 Power House

Let me start off by explaining the words *"Power House."* These words were first documented with the *Xerox 5090 Copier / Duplicator* because early statements cited seven computers controlling this copier. I won't challenge this statement, but I will say there were seven very large microprocessors, talking to each other that controlled the *Xerox 5090 Copier / Duplicator* which I was responsible for.

My manager George mentioned to me that I was to install a *Master Computer (Xerox Automated Test #9 or XAT-9)* for testing the *5090 Power House Copier / Duplicator* seven microprocessors. He stated this, "It Will be a No Brainer" and that it worked flawlessly in the *Xerox Computer Laboratory.* When George said "No Brainer" I believed him and thought I would be on easy street, but at the same time I had an uneasy feeling. (Always plan for the worst.) This *Master Computer* would check well over 9000 circuit steps and the seven microprocessors would be communicating to each other in proper order. The new *Master Computer* was a monster, its size was 2½ feet by about 3½ feet and about 7 feet high. It would have its own air conditioning unit to keep everything at 72 degrees. Management requested a three-day supply of *5090 Power House* computers for startup. There was no way I would go for that, my request to the floor was for five days' supply – just in case there was a problem. This was based on the fact because *Production Control* was always chasing parts, sometimes twenty pages of shortages daily, for the inventory program, *"Just in Time."*

A few days went by and suddenly, our *Maintenance Department* installed the new *5090 Master Computer* over night without my knowledge…

That morning there was a note on the *Master Computer* stating, "The *XAT-9* in the lab was working fine." I decided to fire it up and test the first *5090* computer, the result was REJECT. I tested another 10 units and all units resulted in random REJECTS. Even when retested, the results did not repeat themselves. My first reaction was it may be "Cross Talk" between Direct Current (DC) and Alternating Current (AC) lines. Removing the outer panels from the *Master Computer*, I could find no visible sign, where AC & DC wires were close. The only thing I did not see were ferrite blocks. This would help if AC/DC lines were close, but that was not the case. This situation now would require input from Samuel (Sam) the *Xerox Laboratory Technician* who was responsible for the *Master Computer XAT-9*. Sam was a genius in the electronic field, without question. One thing that set him apart was his unique electronic knowledge. Reviewing the results, he felt *XAT-9* tolerances with integrated circuits, capacitors, diodes, resisters, etc., which required a normal 10 percent tolerance, should be reduced to a tolerance of say 3 or 5 percent. By reducing the electronic tolerances with components (to a more precise measurement) he felt this should enable compatibility with other components. To go in this direction, the production testing would have been set back at least eight or nine months. I showed appreciation with his thinking, and I wanted my thoughts to gently fit in. I also thought the only way forward was to understand the problem, not to second guess it.

I recognized neither of us had an answer to the compelling random data problem with the *Xerox Master Computer*. It looked like there was no path forward, the data was useless, and it had a chilling effect. I needed to show appreciation, but at the same time be persistent, so I could concentrate on my own thoughts. Above all, my objective was to get to the root cause of the problem. I needed to foster cooperation with Sam, encourage his activity, maintain a positive effort and influence... or inspire his thinking. This appeared to be more than a complex problem; however, I was not ready to abandon my initial thinking with electrical cross talk. There was nothing I could tell management that would be beneficial. I was straight forward, but with a bit of tactfulness.

I went home that night after 11:00 pm and I decided to get out a book on electronic interference. I went to bed at almost 3:00 am without any knowledge that would help. Some engineers thought I had inherent abilities for resolving problems. I couldn't account for those inherent abilities. There was nothing in the data that I could dissect or analyze from the *Xerox Master Computer*. How can you organize thoughts and create a specific plan when you have nothing to go on? I could not identify the problem, and all of this had no end in sight. This was a failure at its best, I had to focus on my original thoughts of "Cross Talk." My strongest belief always was, "Failure is not an option."

The next morning after a sleepless night, this was a repeat of the day before, and my energy was being sapped. Sam decided to test another 10 units, and the results again were at random. Most noteworthy we were staring at an avalanche of data that meant nothing to us. It was beyond debate, the same unit tested four different times produced different rejects each time and would not repeat an earlier reject number. Sam and I had nothing to go on. Endeavors with the conditions were eroding, and I needed to keep Sam focused on resolution. We had longer discussions, and to break up the atmosphere, sharing our knowledge was the best resource. Both of us were reaching out to help each other to keep our endurance and sanity intact. Nevertheless, this looked like a major crisis. You can't adhere to or push engineering basics when you have no knowledge of the root cause. To be positive, our key to effectiveness was being <u>good</u> <u>natured</u> to each other.

That afternoon I called my wife and mentioned I would be late again. She understood and often reminded me, my work at *Xerox Corporation* came first. At about 8:15 pm I decided to get a cup of coffee and some chips, since I missed my evening meal. I was on the production floor at a workstation having my coffee and snacks when I noticed something shiny between two boxes on the floor. Being under a table and being between two boxes was exceptional or strange. This was about twenty feet directly in front of me. It seemed unusual to see something like this between the two boxes, so I decided to investigate. Under the boxes was an unattached copper ground rod about five feet long. A copper ground rod is nothing but a steel rod with a copper coating. Not much value except for use as an electrical ground rod. In checking the # 4 ground wire on the back side of the *Xerox XAT-9 Master Computer*, the *Maintenance Department* (installers) did not use the ground rod. However, the bored hole was there from the old computer. The installers hooked up the #4 ground wire to an "I" beam that supported the roof about twenty acres in size. I had the biggest antenna in the world hooked up to the *Xerox Master Computer*. This was picking up radio signals (cross talk) from busses, taxies, police and fire vehicles, airplanes, and short wave etc. I decided to grab that unattached ground rod and put it in my office behind the filing cabinet where no one would see it.

The next morning, I called Sam and requested him to look at the backside of the *Xerox Master Computer*. He found nothing wrong. I mentioned to him to look at the ground cable. Again, he found nothing wrong. I pointed out the ground cable was connected to the "I" beam which supported the roof of twenty acres in size, which was an antenna to the *Xerox Master Computer*. Basically, he then said "Oops!"

A plan was developed to install the ground rod after hours when no one was around. If we had to go back to the *Xerox Maintenance Department*, (our installers) they would then have to have an engineer look at what was done, order a clamp, then schedule a work order which would take more than likely 3 to 4 weeks. Sam had everything we needed in the *Xerox Technical Laboratory*. It was after 11:00 pm (when no one was around) before we could modify the #4 ground wire and install the ground rod with the clamp. While installing the ground rod I noticed it did not take very much force to push the rod into the ground under the floor. I decided to pull the ground rod back up and noticed it was wet. Sam was a little apprehensive about the water. I stated, "No problem, a little water will help with conductivity." He accepted that. We tested about ten of the previous rejects and all passed the *Xerox Master Computer's,* 9000 + circuit tests. It was just after 1:30 am, and we could now go home and get some much-needed rest.

The next morning the *Xerox Master Computer* was running fine, and George a *Xerox 5090 Production Manager* asked, "What was the problem?" My response was "Cross Talk," and I never mentioned the ground rod.

Then two days later, I was met at the front door by an engineer who stated, "The floor was flooded in the *5090 Xerox Master Computer* area. The supervisor on the floor called *Maintenance* to clean up the water." Suddenly, I have another problem. The air conditioner Samuel installed had an (estimated) five-gallon reservoir... of course, it overflowed. I called Sam again and requested input. Sam stated, "To install a pump it would cost ten thousand dollars and my manager would not sign off on that type of work order because of the cost." The reason for rejection was the water had to be pumped up toward the ceiling and then fifty feet or more to a roof drain. A verbal request was made to Sam to make a stainless-steel drain. Sam did an excellent job of manufacturing the stainless-steel reservoir for the air conditioner. Then he could surely make up some stainless-steel fittings with a quick disconnect and run a short stainless line directly into the hole in the floor with the ground rod. This had to look very professional, and you might say it was objective driven with cooperation with

Sam, without paperwork. Sometimes you just need to act without management or maintenance involved. Again, Sam came through, but it was well after midnight when we finally finished and left for a good night's rest.

Then ten months later, I went to work finding the floor was flooded... yes again. Oops, this was big time, water was all over the place. I called Sam again, and I needed an excuse. The timing coincided with the third week of May 1972. Our response to management was, *"Hurricane Agnes overflowed the Artesian Stream under the floor."* Management said nothing, sometimes you are better off keeping some data to yourself.

The *Xerox 5090 Copier / Duplicator* was engineered to exceed the customers' highest expectations. It was a premiere duplicating system with high quality copies.

"If you are taking on a project, know the facts,
real, certain, and actual and never second guess."

Donald A. Drexler

Senior Engineer
5090 Mid Volume Copier / Duplicator
Xerox Corporation

Chapter XX - A Purge of Polychlorinated

Biphenyls (PCBs)

When I was working with the *5600 Mid Volume Copier,* I was requested to purge all *PCBs* in the *Production Line.* This was a massive undertaking requiring design input. Within four weeks I had a massive list of production items to review. This list included: voltage regulators, switches, bushings, electromagnets, electrical insulators and oil-in capacitors (motor starters). These were only some of the items we needed to verify.

This all started with the *Toxic Substance Control Act of 1976* and directed by the *U.S. Environmental Protection Act of 1976.* This act stated once the *PCBs* were removed, we could only replace them with *non-PCBs.*

If we replaced them with a *PCB*, then by *Federal Law, Xerox* was required to place a very large sign on the front of the *Xerox Product* that this machine contained *PCBs, Hazardous Materials.* This type of sign would not help with "customer satisfaction" to say the least. To do something like this would not be in my vocabulary or in the best interest of *Xerox Corporation.* Also, I wanted to ensure federal compliance.

PCBs belonged to a broad family of man-made organic chemicals. These were domestically manufactured from 1929 until manufacturing was banned in 1979. Chemical harm to humans and the environment was widespread. The contamination was overwhelming which contributed to the banning by the *Federal Government.* The studies of *PCBs* in humans found increased rates of melanomas, liver cancer, gall bladder cancer, biliary tract cancer, gastrointestinal tract cancer and brain cancer.

With an analysis, my plan was to identify every *PCB* part and notify the buyer what was "coming down the road." To say the least, it was an intensive review. I needed patience in my decision making with a concern to protect the *Xerox* image.

The design community was going full bore to get drawings created (new part numbers) then *Production Control* would handle the cut-in. I mentioned to *Management* the only way to dispose of *PCBs* was with high temperature incineration. *Design* mentioned there was a plan to get rid of them, but I was unaware of the status.

Everything went fine, but then a year later, I was requested to support / trouble shoot the *Xerox 9900 High Volume Copier.*

I received a visit one day from Vince, a *Senior Electrical Designer*, he was a brilliant person with an excellent electrical background, requesting that we use *PCBs* in the *5600 Mid Volume* copier. My answer was, "No" and I pointed out *Federal Law* and what *Xerox* would have to do. I was tactful in not allowing *PCBs* to be used. I was firm to *"Protect the Xerox Image."* I could not inspire him to think differently, apparently, he was getting directions from upper management, but not his.

A week later I tried to call Vince, the *Senior Electrical Designer* and I was unable to contact him. A few days later I was told he was no longer with *Xerox Corporation*. Vince was a distinguished and keenly intelligent electrical engineer. I was shocked to hear he left the company.

Another week later, I found out that *Xerox Parts Rehabilitation and Spares* (*PR&S*) wanted to use recycled *PCBs* in the *Xerox 5600 Mid Volume Copier*. I suspected this mindset was coming from the *Manager of Parts Rehabilitation and Spares.*

Soon thereafter the overall *Manager of the 9900 High Volume Copier* requested that I sit in on the *Xerox Monthly Management Meetings* in building 208 Webster, New York. I suspected this strategy was deliberate to draw me into a plan where *Parts Rehabilitation and Spares* could apply leverage. What I suspected was right on the money. I was persistent in my *"Path Forward for Xerox."* I was assertive, tactful, and determined to stay the course, however then, conditions were eroding. Directly across from my seat at the table was the *Manager of Parts Rehabilitation and Spares.* This situation was not exactly friendly, and I had a sense of growing uneasiness.

I needed time; I felt a *PR&S* proposal with the use of *PCBs* would be given to my *manager of the 9900 High Volume Copier.* We already had one employee that was no longer with *Xerox Corporation,* and I was not about to change my mind or even think about some type of compromise.

Just over a week later, Eugene the *Xerox 9900 High Volume Copier Manager* came over to me and mentioned *Xerox Parts Rehabilitation and Spares* wanted to use *PCBs* in the *Xerox 5600 Mid Volume* copier. I mentioned *Federal Law* and the consequences with a sign on the front of the copier stating that this machine contains *PCBs, Hazardous Materials.* What then would the customer think? Before he could say anything, I said, "I will take care of it." This was exactly what I wanted.

I reached out by calling the *Manager of the Xerox Legal Department at Xerox Square* and requested his top *Legal Lawyer* get involved. Within minutes my phone rang, and I had the *Senior Legal Lawyer* involved and he understood the consequences. Matter of fact, he faxed me copies of what was happening in the *United States.* I was shocked at what the *Environmental Protection Agency* was doing, and the very large fines being levied.

A week later, I received a letter stating what *Xerox Corporation* could do with *PCBs.* This letter from the *Xerox Legal Department* strongly supported *Federal Law,* and a very large distribution was included.

Needless to say, the *Xerox Parts, Rehabilitation and Spares Division* which attempted to use *PCBs* were very quiet.

*"A Good Path Forward will always require Assertiveness,
Tactfulness and Determination to Stay the Course."*

Donald A. Drexler

*Senior Engineer
High Volume Copier / Duplicator
Xerox Corporation*

CHAPTER XXI - Transport Roll Deflection

The weekly report from *Xerox Final Run and Test* stated two machines had unusual wear with bearing spacers on a transport assembly. I decided to visit *Final Run and Test* and talk to the *Supervisor* and the *Final Run and Test Operators*. In discussions I found out this problem was ongoing with the *Manufacturing Engineer predecessor(s)* for over the course of about three years.

In reviewing the *Manufacturing Engineering* files there was no evidence of a problem. I decided to reach out and visit the *Extended Run Operations*. They knew of the problem, but not recently. Apparently, it was considered normal wear and there was no justification to take further action.

A week later *Xerox Final Run and Test* reported two more machines had bearing thrust wear. On visiting the *Final Run and Test operators*, I requested to see the worn thrust washers. They were thrown away. Now I know this is not going away. Once a *Final Run and Test Union Operator* finds what he considers a problem, it spreads like *"Wildfire"* to everyone in *Final Run and Test*. I suspect this will then turn into a systemic situation, if you were to challenge the union test operators' thinking.

In discussions with the *Xerox Area Manager*, there were previously seven managers (and unknown how many engineers) involved with the *New Build Operation (NBO) Vice President,* all without results.

It's very difficult to justify a problem without evidence or facts. I would follow through with this anyway. A transport assembly was set up in the lab (with and without the belts). The tension with the belts caused the drive roll to deflect about a thirty-second of an inch (.031"). Belt tension was now justification to re-approach the *Xerox Design Department.*

I returned to the *Xerox Design Department* with my results. In reaching out, I could not influence them to act, even with supporting facts. It was evident, I was going nowhere.

The following week, conditions eroded in *Xerox Final Run and Test*, and now, there was a problem in *Extended Run and Test*. I decided again to visit the *Xerox Design Department* and was turned down by three levels of management.

Since being over the above course, and not getting the support, I decided to contact the *Xerox Tiger Team in Fairport, New York*. The *Tigers and Tech Reps* were very aware of the thrust wear problem and were supplied with extra thrust washers whenever they went out. I was sure now I could influence the *Xerox Design Department*.

My initial strategy was tactful and straight forward without success.

I went back to the *Xerox Design Department* and mentioned what was going on with the *Tigers and Tech Reps*. I thought this would be an unprecedented *pivotal point.* Using the *Tigers and the Tech Reps* as leverage didn't work. Apparently, the *Xerox Design Department* didn't understand, "what was on the horizon." I needed to check my vitals.

Having *Xerox Final Run and Test* along with *Xerox Extended Run* reporting thrust wear, it was brought to Eugene, the *Area Managers* attention.

The *Area Manager* asked, "What's going on with the deflection problem?"

In keeping my sanity, I responded by stating, "The detail and facts in acknowledging the thrust failure with the *Xerox Design Department* was at a stalemate. They would not react."

The *Area Manager* then said, "What can we do?"

My response was, "I will need two or three days, let me pursue another avenue of approach."

Why I Wasn't Fired at Xerox

I called the *Vice President's secretary* with the *Xerox Design Division* and requested what the *Vice President's* schedule was for the next day. I was advised of his itinerary, and the best time I might see him was around 10:00 am the next day, when he returned from a meeting. Let's just say I had a good rapport with the *Xerox Vice President and his secretary.*

The *secretary* would always honor my requests, it was evident I was a key person.

The next morning, I was in the building close to the *Vice President's* office, and Everitt the *Vice President* was entering the building. He saw me and asked, "What am I doing over here?"

My response was, "I have some problems with some of your people."

I just happened to have one of the transports with the deflection problem with me. It weighed about eight pounds and had very sharp punch press edges on the legs.

The *Vice President's* response was, "Come into my office, I want to hear about this."

On entering his office, he seated himself behind a highly polished *African Mahogany* desk, and said, "What's the problem?"

My response was, "A roll deflection problem caused by belt tension that prematurely wore out the thrust washers." I mentioned if they would use *"self-aligning bearings"* this would not happen.

His response was, "I don't understand why, they don't want to fix this."

Now, he wants to see the transport assembly and with hands on.

I said to him, "Please put paper down on your desk, because the bottom legs have very sharp edges."

He grabbed the assembly, set it down on his desk, and at the same time, pulled it over close to him and put *"Railroad Tracks"* deep into his polished *African Mahogany* desktop.

I said, "Everitt, look what you have done."

His response was, "I will have it refinished before the week is over."

At that same time my sixth sense kicked in. By his reflex, without words I knew this would be his opportunity to act. I didn't have to say anything.

We then had social conversations with coffee and cookies.

On returning to the *New Build Operation,* while I was still outside, the *Area Manager* saw me approaching and came out on the sidewalk and asked, "Have you made any headway with the *Deflection Problem?"*

My response was, "I've been through three levels of management without results, but I am pursuing other avenues of approach."

We walked into the building and were in the aisle outside of our offices, discussing other problem strategies, when Hans the *Xerox Quality Control Manager* saw us from eighty feet away.

He immediately came over and said, *"The Xerox Design Department* is signing up to make changes for the *Deflection Problem."*

I stated, "I just came from there and I was turned down."

He repeated his statement, and I again said the same as before.

He then said, "It came down from a manager, from several levels of management, and I don't know how far up it started."

The *Xerox New Build Operation, Area Manager* looked at me, and I could detect what he was thinking, "What did I do and how did I pull this off?"

Why I Wasn't Fired at Xerox

I called the *Xerox Design Department* and they stated they didn't fully understand the problem. I mentioned, "there were another ten "design problems" in the *New Build Operation Division* that needed to be addressed. Some of these design problems went back three years or more. I was not going to deal with them, because they had not acted on this and ten other problems. Yet now with some higher-level cooperation, the pressure was on these designers to finally address the issues.

They said, "Bring them over."

The next day, I took all the design problems to them, and they signed up for everything. There seemed to be an urgency to get me out of their office.

On returning to my *New Build Office*, I made copies with all the *"Design Problems"* (indicated on the *Discrepant Material Request*) and left copies on the *New Build Operations (NBO) Area Managers* desk.

A half hour later, the *NBO Area Manager* came over to me and said, "We've had a lot of people work on these problems including our *Vice President*, without results, and you come along and resolve all of them. How did you do it?"

I looked him straight in the eye and said, "It might be my presence." (At that time, I was 6'4" and weighed 250 lbs. I didn't have to carry a big stick).

Now, as *Paul Harvey* would say, "Let me tell you the rest of the story."

The *Design Vice President* came from the same very small coal mining town in *Pennsylvania* as my wife. My wife's sister used to walk (the now *Xerox Design Vice President*) to school. My wife's mother's maiden name just happened to be the same name as the *Vice President's*.

Donald A. Drexler

*"I always wanted to protect the Xerox Image
and the word inaction, was not in my Dictionary."*

Donald A. Drexler

*Senior Engineer
High Volume Copier / Duplicator
Xerox Corporation*

Chapter XXII - A Massive Roll Failure at a Cost of Over $ 1,000,000.^{00}

All of a sudden, the *Hi-Volume Copier/Duplicator, Final Run and Test* operators were reporting critical pressure roll failures. I immediately suspected debonding of the core. I alerted Sebastian the *Xerox Buyer*, who purchased these parts from the Josh Rubber Company in Maryland and immediately headed to the *Document Center* to get roll assembly prints for *Receiving Inspection*. I received the prints and obtained six virgin parts (in sealed boxes from *Fabrication Manufacturing in Webster New York*). These rolls came from the *New Build Operation (NBO) in Webster, New York.* I transported the parts (by my own car) and delivered them directly to *Receiving Inspection*. I expected that the *Inspector,* a union person, would blow me in, because I did not get a union person to carry the parts from the *New Build Operation* to *Receiving Inspection*. If I requested a union person to carry the parts, it would not have happened until the next day.

I requested Dennis, the *Senior Inspection Engineer* to immediately set up inspection for these rolls as an "Emergency." He understood, if I requested this as an emergency it was evident there was a serious problem.

The Inspection set-up was simple; two V-blocks and a dial indicator on a surface plate. The specification for runout was .020" maximum. The first roll measured .065" run-out or 325% out of specification. All the other rolls measured no less than .040" run-out, of specification. This did not look good.

My next step was to contact the *Fabrication Manufacturing Engineer* to trigger a *Purge* of the system. I left an emergency message on his recorder.

The next step was to find as many of the pressure rolls as possible to keep *Final Run and Test* going by *"Leap Frogging"* (I coined the phrase). *Leap Frogging* is testing the machine with an acceptable or inspected roll and when the test is complete, then removing it and assembling it in the next waiting machine to be tested. The finished tested machine would then be shipped to the warehouse with a note, *Missing Pressure Roll number xxx.*

I was able to find sixteen acceptable rolls in the *Manufacturing Lab* and placed them on a cart in the lab that evening at about 8:45 pm. I missed my evening meal that day and was extremely tired and hungry. All I wanted to do was get home for food and some sleep. Early the next morning I found the rolls thrown on the floor, the cart was apparently stolen, it looked to me, that the cart was disassembled, to get it out of the building. The thieves left some of the cart hardware behind. None of the rolls could be used because of sustained damage. I couldn't imagine what my manager was going to say when he heard about this.

The next day I had no feedback with the purge from the *Fabrication Manufacturing Engineer.* I tried calling him – no answer. Stopped by his office and left a note, I needed *Fabrication Engineering* support immediately with the rolls to keep the line from shutting down "by any means." This meant if we had to take good rolls from the warehouse machines to be shipped, we would do it. We were taking on a new meaning with testing our product. My *New Build Management* was aware of and approved my decisions.

I called Sebastian, the *Xerox buyer* and stated the circumstances. I requested the buyer to get a small shipment of rolls. He stated I would have to provide him with a *Deviation* to use *"Out of Specification rolls."* Since the buyer knew, I would have to use defective (out of specification pressure rolls) then he was aware that something else was going on. That was his Freudian slip. My response to his request was, "I would not use

150

Out of Specification rolls." I did that once for a limited number and the implications turned out to be a *"Nightmare."* There was no justification to do it again and I would not play by his rules.

The next day I tried calling the *Fabrication Manufacturing Engineer*, but no answer. Again, I stopped by his office and left another note, I needed immediate support with the *Pressure Roll Purge.*

That afternoon I thought I would make a challenge to do something novel, that would create energy within *Receiving Inspection.* If I could pull this off, it would be a brilliant move. I wished I learned to play chess.

I went to *Xerox Receiving Inspection in Webster, New York* and met with Dennis, the *Senior Engineering Inspector.* This fellow was cognizant of and well versed with the *Xerox Inspection Instruction Manual* with over forty years' experience.

I mentioned to him, I was not getting support from the *Fabrication Manufacturing Engineer* for a *Purge.* I showed Dennis the dates and times I called or stopped by his office and left notes. I needed Emergency help with a *Purge.*

He stated, "That's your problem." It was my problem because *Fabrication Manufacturing Engineering* stated, their quality was so good they did not have to support my *New Build Operation* with *Inspection or Inspection Funding.* Therefore, I was responsible for getting the *Fabrication Manufacturing Engineer* involved.

My response was, "Well, what about *Supplier Quality Assurance*, shouldn't they be involved?"

His answer was, "Yes."

My response was, "Who do you report to?"

His response was, "Victor."

My next question was, "Who does *Supplier Quality Assurance* report to with Josh Rubber Company?" (Now you might say, I was feeding a tail into the wringer).

His response was, "Victor."

My next statement was, "Shouldn't then Victor, know about this?"

I detected the look on his face was not pleasant. He took a copy of the dates and times when I contacted the *Fabrication Manufacturing Engineer* and went into Victor's office. My sixth sense just kicked in. I decided to walk to the farthest corner of the *Receiving Inspection* office. I could hear Victor chewing out someone from 90 feet away, apparently, he was on the phone with *Fabrication Engineering Management*.

The *Senior Receiving Inspection Engineer* came to me and said, "You will be getting a call within the hour." This was unprecedented and I could see Dennis, the *Senior Receiving Inspection Engineer* was considerably stressed. I knew Victor could apply very effective leverage.

A massive *Purge* was underway with over 9000 known parts in Webster, New York. A *Xerox Field Purge* (National) would also be in the works.

Shortly later, I received a call from the *Senior Receiving Inspection Engineer,* and he stated.

1   The *Xerox Buyer,* Sebastian, is on board.

2   The Josh Rubber Company will be in *Webster, New York* tomorrow morning with their personnel to work on the *Purge* in the *Webster Receiving Inspection Department.*

3   The *Webster Receiving Inspection Department* would be putting up a tarpaulin in their department, so union workers would not see the Josh Rubber Company personnel doing work on site.

4   *Xerox Supplier Quality Assurance* has stated they are not knowledgeable of what happened.

When I heard the above item #4, I immediately thought about "Something else is going on."

Early the next morning I checked with Dennis the *Senior Receiving Inspection Engineer,* and he stated, "100% of the assemblies were defective (in a sample of about 150 assemblies)." It was now evident we had a crisis developing on our hands. I quickly estimated the Josh Rubber Company would be here over a month to inspect the balance.

That morning the *Xerox Buyer, Xerox Supplier Quality Assurance,* and the Josh Rubber Company (VP, and the Quality Control Manager) were in my office for a meeting. Introductions were very cordial, and the VP of Josh Rubber Company offered to take my wife and I to dinner that evening. (This was nothing more than a deliberate plan that would compromise my work ethics, and I would have nothing to do with this type of activity.)

I then said, "No thank you" very firmly.

The *Xerox buyer* then stated I would have to sign off on a *"Deviation"* and use defective parts, to keep the *Xerox Production Line* going.

My response to that was, "I would not sign off on a *"Deviation"* to use defective parts." It seemed the buyer was obsessed and determined to force me to use out of specification parts.

The buyer then said, "You signed off once before, you are going to have to do it again." (I knew what kind of a game he was playing).

I again said, "I would not sign off on a *"Deviation"* to use defective parts. *Xerox* was receiving "<u>parts</u> <u>to</u> <u>print</u>" three to four weeks ago, what happened with the process? Josh Rubber Company must be doing something different."

The buyer then pulled out the deviation that, I once allowed a small quantity of defective parts to be used in *Final Run and Test.* (The consequences and implications of using those parts were a disaster.)

I then said, "Take look at my signature, notice I circled my name a few times, that's because, I would not have anything to do with the rest of the signatures on that deviation."

The *Xerox Buyer,* Sebastian then said, "You are going to have to use these parts." It was obvious the buyer had a deliberate plan with what he was trying to do and this was not in the best interest of *Xerox Corporation.*

I then said to the *Xerox Buyer, "If I can't obtain parts to print, then you had better get another supplier."* This was stated in front of the supplier. It was enough to "*Force my Hand*" and the meeting was over.

On leaving my office, the VP of Josh Rubber Company said, "Is there anything we can do?"

My response to that was, "Yes, come to think of it, there is." They immediately stopped, turned toward me and I then finished my statement, by saying, "Just make parts to print."

As they were leaving the building, I noticed the *Xerox Buyer* was saying something to the VP of Josh Rubber Company. I suspected they would do anything to override me.

A footnote to the above sentence. I had heard Josh Rubber Company had given paid vacation trips to Bermuda for *Xerox* buyers / production control personnel and was offering scholarships paid to colleges directly, for youth. These people were doing business, not in the best interest of *Xerox Corporation.* I would never tolerate this type of business or activity.

It was evident that the buyer was trying to force me to use defective pressure rolls for a reason. I could not understand why the buyer was persistent in forcing me to use defective pressure rolls. I suspected the buyer was very much involved with greed and the supplier was not offering a cost reduction to *Xerox Corporation*. I would not play by his rules. There is a serious question of <u>trust</u> when a buyer tries to force engineering to use defective parts. What the buyer is attempting to do does not support the *Xerox* image. I also detected some vindictiveness in his manners. Could it be higher stakes for himself?

One of the things I mastered at *Xerox* was an "additional sense." If I had to ask a question, before anything was said, I could tell in which direction (by facial reactions) we were going in a fraction of a second.

I immediately called the *Xerox Program Design Manager* and mentioned what transpired minutes before in my office. Later that day, the *Design Manager* mentioned to me they tried to get him to over-throw my decision. He would not have anything to do with their mindset.

I discussed a special plan with the *High-Volume Area Manager*. I first stated, "I would have to shut his production line down." I thought he was going to come apart, but I got his attention. This portion of the plan would be mentioned to the *Buyer* and *Production Control*.

Another portion of my plan would only be known with the *Xerox High-Volume Area Manager* along with *Final Run and Test*. I was able to obtain three union workers to go to the *Xerox* warehouse to remove pressure rolls to be used in the *Xerox Final Run and Test Department* to keep the *Production Line* going. I had just enough pressure rolls to keep the *Final Run and Test* operating. This is referred to "Leap Frogging" as mentioned earlier in this chapter.

Because of my knowledge in the field (the customer's office), the pressure roll would cause trail edge wrinkles on the copy and copy quality would then be at its worst. If the results for roll runout (out of round) was more than specification, then the roll would prematurely debond in test because of temperature coupled with pressure.

Because of my analytical thinking a massive problem would be eliminated. I realized very quickly that I was contributing to yet another historic moment in *Xerox* history.

That evening there was a meeting with Eugene in the *High-Volume Area Manager's* office, and I was not invited by plan. I was in the plant, on the *High-Volume Production* floor until after 11:00 pm. This meeting was with the *Xerox Buyer, Xerox Management, Supplier Quality Assurance* (*SQA*) and the VP of Josh Rubber Company. From what I was told the next day, the *High-Volume Area Manager* backed my decisions entirely. I was pleased to hear everything went well.

Four days later I was leaving the *New Build High-Volume Building 200* about 6:40 pm and I was in the parking lot near my car. I heard a projectile whistling directly over my head and a fraction of a second later heard the gunshot fired. The shot was fired from the woods across *Caracas Drive* on the north side of *Xerox Building 200*. This was a hi-velocity 22 caliber long rifle round. The velocity of that type of projectile was estimated at around 1400 per second, much faster than the speed of sound. That type of round is inaccurate and would be high if sighted in with standard ammunition.

My first reaction was someone in the woods does not know or understand safety and responsibility with firearms. Firing a shot in the direction of a building and a parking lot is unthinkable and is totally unsafe. If there would have been more than the one shot, I would have called the *New York State Police*. I thought no more of it.

Certified pressure rolls were being supplied by *Xerox Supplier Quality Assurance (SQA)*, especially for the copier/duplicators in the warehouse.

Four weeks later I was trying to contact the *Xerox Buyer*, Sebastian, and no one answered his phone.

Talking to the *High-Volume Area Manager*, I stated I was not able to contact Sebastian the *Xerox Buyer*.

He stated, "You don't know what happened?"

I said, "I don't know what you are talking about."

He again stated, "You don't know what happened?"

I again said, "I don't know what you are talking about."

I then detected a concerned look on his face.

He then said, "Come over to my office."

At his office he requested me to close the door.

The High-Volume Area Manager, stated at the end of the meeting four weeks earlier, the *Xerox Buyer* stood up on a chair, lifted his fist and said, *"I am going to kill Don Drexler."* Saying this in front of *SQA, Xerox Management,* and the supplier Josh Rubber Company was a mistake.

The next day he was no longer employed with *Xerox Corporation.*

The purge evidence was overwhelming with a 100% reject rate. Over 9000 pressure rolls had to be returned to Josh Rubber Company at a cost of over $1,000,000. [00]

Josh Rubber Company would replace the pressure rolls with *Xerox Supplier Quality Assurance* certified assemblies.

Apparently, the Josh Rubber Company knew what was going on and then in a few weeks corrected their manufacturing process.

About that same time frame, Eugene the *High-Volume Area Manager* gave me a post-it note with a phone number. I said, "What's this about?" He said, "I don't know." Coming from a high-level manager, I suspected something from above was about to impact my territory.

I called the number and was talking to the *Secretary of the Vice President of High Volume.*

I mentioned, "What's this about?"

The *Secretary's* response was, "I can't talk about this over the phone."

I then said, "I am going to say two words, your answer should be either yes or no… Was it the Pressure Roll?"

Her response was, "Yes."

My response was, "I know which file to bring."

In a meeting with the *Xerox Vice President of High Volume* he asked the question, "Why were we were paying over $1,000,000.^{00} for rework of the pressure rolls?"

I then handed him the documentation (a *Supplier Discrepant Materials Report*) signed by the Josh Rubber Company that the supplier (Josh Rubber Company), had agreed to rework the parts at "no cost" to *Xerox Corporation.*

The *V.P.* then said, "Could this be a mistake or is this deliberate?"

My response was "I can't answer that question." I also mentioned someone should look into this, there is too much going on and I shared some detail with him."

It was now the *Xerox Vice President's* turn to resolve why we should pay such a large bill from Josh Rubber Company for over a $ 1,000,000. ^{00} and investigate what else was going on.

Our *V.P.* was aware of some suppliers giving *Xerox buyers* very large gifts. Some were paid vacations in the *Bahamas* with everything paid for, room, board, food, and golfing. I also was aware of *Xerox* workers being offered college scholarships paid directly to the schools. This was greed at the worst level you could think of.

After about seven weeks the *High-Volume Copier/Duplicator Production* in the *New Build Operation* finally came back to normal.

Josh Rubber Company was making parts to print with *Xerox Supplier Quality Assurance* involved.

Then, months later there was a massive layoff in the buyer's community.

I will let you connect the dots.

Why I Wasn't Fired at Xerox

"When you have out-of-control situations,
You must maintain:
Common sense, a good attitude, endurance,
patience, commitment, and determination."

Donald A. Drexler

Senior Engineer
High Volume Copier / Duplicator
Xerox Corporation

Donald A. Drexler

Chapter XXIII - Timing Chain Setting

The operators in *Xerox Final Run and Test* were reporting the timing chain was too tight and others were saying it was too loose.

I was aware of this problem and thought that my predecessor(s), the *Xerox High Volume Manufacturing Engineers* were slow to do anything about it. The *Xerox Design Engineers* were laughably inconsistent at times. I can only say this now. Of course, it would take a *Xerox Engineering Change Notice* to fix it. Apparently, the timing chain issue came up again, in *Final Run and Test or Extended Run* and it was cited as a *Xerox Design* problem.

Now, when the *Final Run and Test* union operators pick up on something like this, almost all of them are going to say, yep, "it's too tight" or "it's too loose," maybe some will say "it's perfect." Of course, then the extremes will spread like "Wildfire." Yes, of course they are all right. *The Amalgamated Clothing and Textile Workers Union* in the *Final Run and Test* were 100% right this time, with different answers.

If you look at the overall design of the serpentine chain, the many sprockets, and the newness of the working parts, you should consider a break-in period. But that was only a small part of the problem. Then you need to consider tolerances, true position and run out. True position and run-out are the throttlers. You can lose your sanity if you decide to try and solve it by mathematics. Because of true position and run out with many sprockets, the chain tension at various, tangency points with the sprockets will be all over the place.

Xerox Design Management assigned Gérard an excellent *Xerox Senior Design Engineer* with many years of experience with *Xerox Corporation*. Gérard decided to look me up for resolution with this problem.

I said to Gérard, "Ok, let's go for a walk." I grabbed a blank *"Xerox Deviation"* form, then said, "Let's stop and get a cup of coffee and a snack in the break area."

During the coffee break I took a napkin and sketched a plan on it to resolve the problem. I detected Gérard was not following me. I would have to show him what I required in the line setting for the chain tensioning.

After the coffee and snack, I took him down to the hardware crib. I required a slightly longer bolt that was used to tighten the idler sprocket, a castellated nut and a Delrin washer. I put a few of each of these items in my shirt pocket. The *Xerox Identification Numbers* for parts were carefully recorded.

I then took Gérard over to the *Manufacturing Assembly Line*, where the idler was assembled with a loaded spring that set the tension with the chain. Once the hardware was tightened the idler did not move. This was stupidity at its best. I removed the bolt and replaced with the longer bolt, placed the Delrin washer between the idler and the frame, torqued the castellated nut to about 12-inch lbs., then backed the castellated nut off about ½ turn. This then allowed the idler to float with the chain, and the spring tension now holding the idler, was free to move in place.

Gérard said to me, "How come we didn't think of this before?"

My response to him was, "That's why I am here."

A *"Xerox Design Deviation"* was processed at the coffee break for cut in. It was up to Gérard to process this with *Design* and through *Production Control*.

I knew that if I tried to process a deviation through *Xerox Production Control* it would not happen.

Xerox Production Control wanted the *Xerox Design Department* on board, for design revisions with the drawings, for their production cut-in control. I thought that they just refused to yield or were stubborn because the process had to match the drawing. A good example was very expensive castings (high volume developer housings) that were modified in the field using whatever hardware was available to make it work. The holes were redrilled and tapped for larger hardware sizes. On reusing these expensive castings, much of the hardware did not match the drawing as *Production Control* wanted it.

I didn't mean to get off the track, but two days later, I checked *Final Run and Test* and the idler was floating perfectly. What *Production Control* didn't know, didn't hurt them.

Only the *Production Assembly Union Person* and the *Supervisor* were aware of this change. The *Xerox Process* was *"Jury Rigged" (impermanent)* with the revised hardware; therefore, *Production Control* had no idea what was in the process, * but the new hardware was clearly specified in the process. If *Production Control* knew what was done, there would have been *"Hell to Pay because the material used didn't match the Print."* I often wondered why we needed *Production Control,* especially when we were always running out of parts with a three-day *"Just-in-Time"* supply.

I verified the idler in *Final Run and Test* was floating properly for about two and a half weeks. I let Gérard know we should get a drawing change.

Just over a month went by and I found out the *"Spring Chain Tension"* in *Final Run and Test* was again a problem.

On checking with *Final Run and Test,* I noticed the idlers were floating as intended.

The only thing I said to the *Amalgamated Clothing and Textile Workers Union, Final Run and Test* inspectors, about their problem was, "I am not reacting, everything is working fine."

The *Final Run and Test* inspectors should have seen the idler moving as intended.

I was hoping they would write me up. But that didn't happen or maybe they knew the idler was floating, and it was a test.

   * If *Xerox Production Control* ever "read" the *Assembly Process Instruction Field* of the *Process Engineering* instructions they would have discovered my method. Their computer only checked the *Assembly Process Parts List Field*, then the *Design Assembly Print*. The *Assembly Process Parts List Field* would always match the print, but the build *Assembly Process Instruction Field* would spell out what we needed or required. *Production Control* would never look at the *Assembly Process Instruction Field*, and only did what their computer told them to do.

Mission "accomplished" by "*Jury-Rigging*" the system.

"To challenge thinking, You need a Strategy, Use Common Sense, Be Straight Forward, Be Sensitive and Precise. Know your facts."

Donald A Drexler

     Senior Engineer
     High Volume Copier / Duplicator
     Xerox Corporation

Chapter XXIV - Mechanical Failure with an

Adjustable Arm

I was assigned many sub-assemblies for the *9900 High Volume Copier-Duplicator*. Most all these sub-assemblies were used in other copiers and duplicators. In one area we had an adjustment arm that I was familiar with, however, I was not the initial *Manufacturing Fabrication Engineer* responsible. I could write a thesis on what "to do or not" that would capture everyone's attention. That engineer was extremely talented in the *Manufacturing Fabrication Milling and Drilling Department* and he took shortcuts to save tooling expense. I looked at the gage, a flush pin gage and said, "How much is the tolerance?" He replied, ".002 thousands inch." I knew the gage was made wrong which then accepted bad parts. He then said, "If my manager ever found out about this, there would be hell to pay because the pin gage I was using did not comply with design practices." He also mentioned a gage with dial indicators would cost about $10,000.^{00}. With my background, I knew his pin gage would work, however the added tolerances with diameter, true position, and angularity this gage would also accept out of specification units. The part, even a rejected one would fall through the gage as an acceptable part. With reconditioned recycled parts this pin gage would not apply, they needed to use a dial indicator. The gage design was mis-applied beyond debate. I would let him play by his rules, and never anticipated I would be responsible for using re-conditioned adjustment arm assemblies in the *High-Volume Copier-Duplicator* down the road.

Nonetheless years later I had the consequences. One or two assemblies found in the *Xerox Final Run and Test* would be rejected. Then more would show up, finally I would obtain those assemblies and take them to the *Xerox Metrology Laboratory* to be inspected. The *Manufacturing Fabrication Department* was not recycling these assemblies, but it was offloaded to a supplier, therefore, I needed to touch base with the *Xerox Buyer*. I received a report from the buyer that all parts were tested "accept." At this point, I had no idea how the assemblies were inspected. Now the proportion of rejects in *Xerox Final Run and Test* was escalating near out of control. More assemblies were taken to the *Xerox Metrology Laboratory* to be inspected and the results were worse than before. I made another call to the *Xerox Buyer* mentioning something was drastically wrong. I asked the *Xerox Buyer* if the supplier was using a pin gage to inspect the parts. The buyer didn't know, but he would find out. The next day I was informed it was a pin gage and I informed the buyer a pin gage is not to be used for tolerances of .002" or less. I mentioned the supplier required dial indicators.

In checking with *Xerox Fabrication Engineering* no dial indicator gage was ever made. My next step was to confront and challenge the *Xerox Tool Designer* for supplying a gage that did not conform to *Xerox Gage Practices 3.2.1.*. I informed the buyer of where we stood, and I was going nowhere unless there was a meeting with everyone. I really wanted to go directly to the *Vice President of Xerox Manufacturing Engineering* because the *Xerox Tool Design Department* reported to him. I estimated gage tooling (dial Indicators) would now cost an estimated $15,000.^{00} or more. My management wanted to wait and see what happened. What I wanted was, to force my hand with the *Vice President of Fabrication Engineering* and have *Xerox Tool Design* pick up the tab because of the disservice they did to *Xerox Corporation*. It was the mindset of *Fabrication Engineering* that caused the current consequences.

Meanwhile the *Xerox Final Run and Test* people were almost tantamount to being out of control, with machine assemblies that did not work. The atmosphere was eroding quickly.

To make matters worse, it was evident the *Xerox Supplier Quality Assurance Team* could not contribute, because <u>critical</u> machining skills would be required. The supplier did not know how to address the very tight tolerances required. With that said, the supplier had no temporary corrective measures in place with this assembly.

I received a call from the *Xerox Buyer,* and he scheduled a meeting in *Parts Rehabilitation and Spares Division,* in their conference room the next day. I mentioned *Xerox Tool Design* must be there along with *Supplier Quality Assurance.*

The meeting was well attended, and a *Senior Tool Designer* was present.

I then asked the *Senior Tool Designer* to explain why a pin gage was supplied as a gage. He had no answer. I then requested him to explain the *Xerox Design Gage Manufacturing Standard of 3.2.1* etc. He explained, "the standard, and for a part or assembly with a tolerance of less than .002" you must use dial indicators with that gage." I then asked, "if *Xerox* had a dial indicator gage for this assembly," and the answer was "no." I then addressed the *Xerox Buyer* and mentioned, "To remanufacture this assembly, *Xerox Tool Design* would require a dial indicator gage along with special tooling. I then turned to the *Senior Tool Designer* and said, "Why wasn't the *Xerox Fabrication Manufacturing Engineering* supplied with this?" I didn't get an answer. I then left the meeting, and I wasn't going to repeat myself. I also felt, I would not be responsible for spending funds for someone else's blunder and misjudgment, or consequences that were deliberate.

I wanted the *Xerox Buyer* and the *Fabrication Engineering Tool Design* to work this out. If not, I would be talking to the *Vice President of Xerox Manufacturing Engineering.*

Within the *Xerox Final Run and Test Department* the time was almost two hours to replace this unit, because of disassembly and reassembly. Then, you don't know if you have an acceptable assembly to replace the defective unit. It is devastating when there is no instant success and there is no path forward. This is where leadership is important and the key to effectiveness is being tactful, good natured and fundamentally straight forward. Also, we need cooperation from everyone.

The *Xerox Buyer* called me the next morning and requested we meet with the supplier. This was because *Xerox Tool Design* would not be cooperative. I would like to say a few words here, but I will hold my temperament. I wanted the *Xerox Buyer* involved, (because there would be a supplier funding request), along with a *Xerox Supplier Quality Assurance* person. He agreed. I requested we meet as soon as possible because of the chaotic situation in *Xerox Final Run and Test.* He understood.

A meeting was set up with the supplier the very next day. On viewing the equipment setup, it was certainly evident we would never get an acceptable assembly. I was starting to think this company does not have the technical ability or the skills to process this type of assembly.

Now, I must be very careful, sensitive, and straight forward with what I would say next. Under the circumstances, I needed to be patient, honest, candid, and tactful. Also being good-natured and friendly would certainly help. At the same time, I wanted to focus on the horizon with *Xerox Management*, because without question we would "continue" to receive some rejects. This would be a game changer and there was only one way to navigate through this disaster.

My proposal to the supplier was, "We would continue to see 30% to 50% rejects." Everybody "just lit up" when they heard this. Well, I got their attention. Most of those parts would still be functional. I then explained, "I believed my risk is somewhere between 3% and 5%. This would be the proportion of rejects in line with binding issues. With this strategy, there would be no guarantees, due to inadequate tooling and gages. If it rose to 10%, then, I would take it up with *Xerox Tool Design* and, if they continued to be non-cooperative, I would go, without question, to the *Vice President of Xerox Manufacturing Engineering*. If *Xerox Manufacturing Fabrication* would supply this assembly, the assembly with gage tooling would be very expensive using dial indicators.

Let me explain what needs to happen.

1)   Any damage to the "mounting hole" with this assembly, then that part was to be scrapped. The *High-Volume Copier-Duplicator Engineering Department* was to be notified if more than five percent are found.

2)   An expanding collet was to be used for location of the boring operation.

3)   A retracting diamond locating pin was to be used for boring true position.

4)   A high-speed boring cutter intended for bronze must be used, with proper primary rake design, using a light feed, say .005."

5)   A soluble oil such as *Master Oil* with a 5% mix would be in the best interest.

6)   If the expanding collet does not hold the part secure, then clamping will be required. If this is done, then true position will be lost.

7)   The expanding collet must be free at all times of fine bronze chips. One small chip would cause a reject in *Final Run and Test*.

Everyone agreed to the above.

The *Xerox High-Volume Copier-Duplicator Engineering Area Manager* was appraised of the approach and agreed.

For many weeks, I did not hear of a binding issue. Yes, we were using many parts "Out of Specification," however, they worked functionally under the circumstances.

"Under circumstances, if you can influence or inspire another person, then do it."

Donald A Drexler

Senior Engineer
High Volume Copier / Duplicator
Xerox Corporation

Chapter XXV - A Feeder Cut-in Rejected

Without a Line Trial Test

I was approached by a *Xerox Design Engineer*, Elliot (fresh out of college) about a cut-in (revision to put into the production line) with a paper feeder device.

I was aware of problems in the feeder area especially with *nip penetration*. Most of these problems were always directed at the *Program Design* because it dealt with paper transfer or movement. I requested to see one print and focus on the tangency contact point.

This part was made of plastic (which I thought was stupid) in the feeder section and there were no revision changes for this part. Therefore, it was just used many times. Finding this critical part as a plastic part, I thought was a major mistake by *Program Design*. The first thought that came to my mind was, "Why didn't the *High-Volume Manufacturing Engineer* predecessor, catch this a long time ago?" The part at a critical contact point at tangency contained a mold parting line. I thought this was a major contributing factor with the *Final Run and Test Section* problems.

Before I would say anything to the *Design Engineer,* I wanted to do a quick tolerance study of the plastic feeder part.

I needed to review tolerances that were controlled by true position, diameter tolerance, next was angularity control and then throw in, out of roundness. In my head I quickly did a tolerance study and came up with an aggregate tolerance that was 400% greater than the setting tolerance.

I said to the *Design Engineer*, "I can't cut this in. The plastic feeder part has four times greater tolerance than my setting tolerance." It appeared he was not reacting with my knowledge or the reported existing paper movement problems (jams, skew or multi sheet feeds).

The *Design Engineer* then said, "You will cut this in."

He then left me with the prints and said, "Goodbye!"

I would have expected that he would have requested a *Line Trial in Final Run and Test*. If that had been attempted, I would have requested a meeting with his manager. I strongly felt any *Line Trial in Final Run and Test* would have been a major waste of time.

I immediately informed my *Copier-Duplicator High-Volume Area Manager* of what transpired. He didn't say one word. I thought that was a little unusual.

Less than three weeks later my *Copier-Duplicator High-Volume Area Manager* showed up at my office at 8:00 am with an *Amalgamated Clothing and Textile Union Worker (Parts Handler)* and he had two thousand parts for cut-in.

I said to my *Copier-Duplicator High-Volume Area Manager*, "What's this all about?"

The *Area Manager* said, "It's a paper feeder device."

My response to that was, "I rejected that almost three weeks ago."

The *Area Manager* said, "Cut these in" and asked me to "look at one of the parts." Each part was in a small box with foam bedding to protect the part. This was not a plastic part but was a brilliantly polished stainless-steel feeder part. Looking it over very carefully, this was a <u>major</u> <u>answer</u> <u>to</u> <u>a</u> <u>massive</u> <u>problem</u>. All I could think of, "This was dumb luck."

I said to the *Area Manager*, "Do you have a drawing?"

The *Area Manager* said, "No."

I then said, "Do you have a part number?"

The *Area Manager* said, "No."

I then said, "Do you have a *Xerox Change Notice?*"

The *Area Manager* said, "No."

I then said, "Do you have a *Deviation*?"

The *Area Manager* said, "No."

I then said, "And now you want me to cut these parts in?"

The *Area Manager* said, "Yes" very firmly.

My sixth sense just kicked in and I suspected action to resolve the issue was coming from above or the *Design High-Volume Area Manager's* office.

Did I trigger this by simply saying, "No to a cut-in?" Sometimes you must have strong suspenders.

I knew how to "rig the system," so that *Production Control* – (Ingrid) would not find out immediately, but then someday she just might. I mentioned to the *Area Manager of the High-Volume Copier-Duplicator*, "If *Production Control* found out about what I was about to do, there would be Hell to Pay."

He said, "Don't worry about it."

I did a small tryout and modified the setting technique. The follow-up in *Final Run and Test* went extremely well with the initial parts. I talked with the *Amalgamated Clothing and Textile Union Operators* in *Final Run and Test*, and a month later they all stated, "All of the problems in the feeder area just disappeared."

After I heard those comments, I celebrated that evening with my wife and some champagne. My wife knew this was one of the "best moments" in my career at *Xerox Corporation*.

Five and a half months later, Ingrid, the *Xerox Production Controller* received a *Xerox Cut-in Notice* with updated drawings and a sample of parts for a *Xerox Line Tryout*. With everything in hand, she went to the *Xerox Supervisor on the Production Floor for the Line Try-Out*. The *Xerox Supervisor* took one look at the parts and said, "Don Drexler cut them in months ago."

From what I heard; you could have scraped her from the ceiling.

The next thing you knew she was in the *Xerox Copier-Duplicator High-Volume Area Manager's* office with a closed-door session. She wanted me fired. I'm sure he made a conscious effort to hear her out.

After she left, he came over to my office, closed the door, sat down, put his elbows up on my table, then put his head in his hands and said, "If I get into trouble, I will want a street fighter like you on my side." We smiled at each other, and I said, "Thank you for that very nice compliment." All it takes is a little laughter to brighten the day up.

What Ingrid did not know; it was the *Vice President of Program Design* that made this happen, I was the "pivot point." I tried to make things right with Ingrid. However, it was difficult for her to understand that I followed instructions from top level management.

"All I wanted to do for Xerox Corporation,
was the right thing to turn the situation around."

Donald A. Drexler

Senior Engineer, High Volume Copier /
Duplicator Xerox Corporation

Chapter XXVI - A Foxboro or IBM Computer

Was Required, However, Ingenuity Prevailed

This is next to the shortest Chapter with my career at *Xerox Corporation*.

My position as a *Senior Engineer* with the *American Customers Operations* was to put together a *Computer Tracking System* that would track parts worldwide for *North, Central and South America*. This was to cover, two *Xerox Copy Machines* (a *Domestic Machine and a Multinational Machine*) that would be built at *Xerox, Beijing, China*.

The *Chinese Domestic Machine* was straight forward. The *Multinational Machines* required voltage variances along with language differences.

I started to put together a plan that would cover *Part or Assembly, Cost, and Tooling* expenses. This would cover quotations for tooling, parts, or assemblies for initial prototype startup, to final production with lead times on a worldwide basis. This system was growing exponentially out of control. I realized there would be variables and unknowns, especially if there was a required snapshot with cost history. We would need to know how the costs were changing over time. This would be challenging, it required patience, perseverance, and persistence to make this work. The very large size of this database was a brutal reality. Being committed, I always believed, "Any barrier could be broken."

This database was very large and had over one hundred and twenty-five basic sorts. Multiple sorts added to the basic sorting would have multiple possibilities, but I wanted to keep my approach simple.

I did not think the basic *Xerox Star Computer* was able to handle a massive amount of data. I was right, the equipment crashed many times. As I talked to my *Manager* Daniel, I requested equipment that could handle very large amounts of data. I suggested an *International Business Machine* or a *Foxboro* computer. This equipment would allow me to also make monthly snapshots for history. This equipment could also be used widely for the entire *American Customer Operation*. The cost was between $350,000 and $375,000 to get one computer. That was turned down.

Now, I needed to rethink my approach. How could I overcome this dilemma?

The answer would be an advanced computer such as the *Xerox RF Computer*. This equipment was rare. My manager was able to bring this equipment on board. From what I was told, this was the only *Xerox RF Computer* in *New York State*. With this unit, I still would have problems with snapshots and sending large amounts of data, especially overseas.

In the 1980s before the internet, the only way to send data electronically overseas was to fax it. Periodically you would get broken signals and then the data was worthless.

I decided to have a discussion with a *Vice President,* with whom I had extremely good relations. You might say this would be a game changer, by whatever means possible. Of course, the means or ways was unorthodox.

Then, within a few days my *Xerox RF Computer* was hooked into the *International Business Machine* mainframe on the *Webster, New York* site.

This equipment worked extremely fine for four-and-one-half years. I never had a problem with the *RF Computer*. Also, I never heard of any billing from the *Computer Complex*.

Suddenly, I was advised I would have to move to the *Henrietta, New York Complex*. I mentioned we were using the *Computer Complex Mainframe* in *Webster, New York,* and I never saw a bill or invoice for use with my *RF equipment*.

I mentioned to my manager, moving my computer would bring light to my *RF Computer* usage, with the *IBM Mainframe,* for four-and-one-half years. I was told, "That was not a problem."

In moving we did get a large bill; however, it was not a problem.

"Focusing on a Goal will enable
you to achieve Your Dream."

Donald A. Drexler

Senior Engineer ~ Xerox Corporation
American Customers Operations
North, Central & South America

Donald A. Drexler

Chapter XXVII - Designed & Installed a

Computer Tracking System

Here is a <u>little</u> <u>history</u> of the *Xerox 8010 Star Information System.*

In May1981, I was assigned a *Xerox 8010 Star Information System.* This was shortly after the computer system was introduced on April 27, 1981. My first thought was this was a glorified mailbox. No other engineers were assigned one, until many months later. Initially the only people I could communicate with were the secretaries (or admins) in the *Xerox Document Center.* This was the <u>first</u> commercial office computer with a mouse. This equipment was innovative and expensive. The computer workstation was set up with a cathode ray tube (CRT), icons, a text editor, graphics program and spreadsheet software.

The Xerox 8010 Star Information System was not intended to be a stand-alone system, but to be integrated as part of a *"Personal Office System."* You would need several *Star Computers* linked together to make full use of them. I initially did not think this system would be able to communicate worldwide in a matter of seconds.

The initial system had:

> 1.4 megabytes of memory
>
> Up to 40 megabytes of local disk storage
>
> 17" display
>
> 8" floppy

The *Xerox 8010 Star Information System* for its time had integrity, innovation, and excellence. This was the first-time computers could be linked together in an office.

These features were revolutionary.

Years later, I was requested to take a position as a *Program, Marking Imaging, Reliability Manager* for the *High-Volume Copier/Duplicator*. I was asked by my *Program Manager* to take a computer class, to learn about programming computers, installing software, hardware etc., I thought this was unusual. I mentioned, I was self-trained, never took a computer course (outside of the *Basic Beginner 8010 Star Computer Course*).

Because of the *Xerox Star Computer* limitations with voluminous workloads, I created the *Xerox Launch Profile Program* for the *American Customer Operation* using a *RF Computer (Ethernet 241) with the IBM Mainframe*. I wrote the entire *RF* system starting with a blank sheet of paper, from software to hardware installation. Apparently, I was good with binary logic. Records would be kept for engineering and procurement for tooling, pre-production, production cost from initial to final production. My area to cover was *North, Central and South America*. Many other countries around the world were involved with all phases of production. The *Launch Profile System* was a very large system and had one hundred and twenty-five basic sorts and worked extremely well with the *IBM* main frame.

This *RF* equipment worked extremely well for four-and-one-half years, until copier launch in *Beijing, China,* in mid-1994. The history is also documented in *Chapter XXVI*.

That being said, "I still had to go to school."

I was requested to bring examples of my work to the *Computer Class*. I mentioned to the *Computer Instructor* that I was also using therobligs for sorting. Therobligs are engineering shorthand for massive engineering problems which identifies a particular item. Because I was good at creative shortcuts the instructor thought it would be beneficial to the class if I shared my thought process. With his modesty he must have been impressed with me as he asked me to teach the remainder of the class. At the end of the course, he thanked me for my willingness to step in. I enjoyed every minute of the course, but teaching was not my calling.

The theroblig name was coined by an instructor at the *Rochester Institute of Technology*, many years ago. These are like "therbligs" used with elemental time and motion, but therobligs (also spelled differently) are a form of engineering shorthand in the computer.

On returning to work in *Webster, New York*, my *Program, Marking Imaging Manager* asked, "How did you make out in the *Computer Class?*"

My response was, "I taught the *Computer Class.*"

He looked at me and said, "What?"

I said, "That's right."

He was astonished and surprised...

"A Good Example Will
Always Inspire Others."

Donald A. Drexler

Marking Imaging Program
Reliability Manager ~ Xerox Corporation

Donald A. Drexler

Chapter XXVIII - An Air Flow Problem With

Refrigeration to Solve It

During *Program* startup with a new high-speed copier/duplicator design for the *Docutech 135* (see Appendix VI), we had an air flow heating problem in the machine, that caused some major concerns. This would be close to the top of my "solution list" as a *Xerox Program Reliability Manager*. However, as a *Reliability Manager*, I would have nothing to do with air flow heating problems requiring refrigeration. I knew that would cause secondary problems.

Before I get into details, let me give you a little background about a small part of my past employment dealing with air.

Early in my career I had the opportunity to work with a highly skilled *Aeronautical Air Flow Designer* named *Fred Lavell*. His interest was in very high-volume air flow. He captured my attention by being motivated, determined, and committed. His hobby and interest were to set a *Land Speed Record*. Knowing and understanding air flow, he had the natural ability to resolve air flow problems. He stated to me one day that he only understood <u>undercarriage</u> <u>air</u> <u>flow</u>. I thought he was being modest saying that, without exception he was an air flow genius. He set a *Land Speed Record* during *Speed Week 1956*. I was honored to have him work for me.

What does his accomplishment have to do with my current problem? You could say he set this record by understanding the following statement extremely well.

"Aerodynamics is the branch of physics, that treats the action of force on bodies in motion."

Whenever he discussed aerodynamics, he captured everyone's attention. I was inspired and influenced by his talks of aerodynamics, especially with reaction time and the forces of resistance.

The aerodynamics physics involved (as stated) will be the answer to the air flow and heat problem. Hang on.

The Problem. Each week, I attended the *Xerox Sunrise Meetings* with the *High-Volume Program Manager*. At each meeting I would submit the most serious problems identified during the week. I maintained a *"Fix / Effectivity"* list until resolved. There were seven managers who worked reliability for me. Two of them thought I was from Missouri (the Show Me State), and knew I wanted to see proof of a fix and how effective it would be. If they did not have the right answers, I would request they prove it to me (show me) in the *Xerox Lab*. They always came up with good resolutions to their problems.

For many weeks we had this heat problem. Every week the *High-Volume Program Manager,* Stanley would bring up refrigeration. I mentioned time and time again, refrigeration was not the answer to a heat problem.

My goal was to utilize the blower-fan from the *9900 High Volume* Copier / *Duplicator,* with computerized programming that performed extremely well for reducing heat problems. For the record, the *Xerox 9900 Duplicator* was introduced on March 7th, 1984, and their blower fan operated with no problems for well over 9 years.

I stated, "If we were to install refrigeration or an air conditioning unit, we would have water to deal with." I also mentioned, "This would require a water pump and a sewer line to be installed or a key operator would have to carry a slop bucket away each day." I just wasn't getting any traction with him.

Well, after hearing this one too many times, I finally said, "Stanley, I can get you refrigeration, with a vortex in the *Xerox Fuser Lab*, that will go to minus forty degrees Fahrenheit, on instrument air, without electricity."

His response was, "That's impossible." Now, I had his attention.

I stated, "I would call his secretary June, next Friday around 10:00 am, and request her to let you know when I have a vortex set up in the *Xerox Fuser Lab*."

The *Xerox Fuser Lab* is one of the hottest rooms in the building with temperatures around 115^+ degrees daily. Whenever you have heat, moisture tends to cease. Using instrument air there should not be moisture in it. I would expect some condensation, because of a significant temperature change within the conduit.

That next Friday, I set up the vortex, and snow was flying in the *Xerox Fuser Lab*. The technician working there noticed the snow and came over to check it out. I warned him not to put his hand anywhere close to the vortex. It would freeze his fingers instantly and he would wind up in the hospital. He understood.

I mentioned to him I needed to go for a walk on the *Xerox Production* floor. I needed a couple pieces of large hardware. The only place I thought I could find them was near the bumper boards that protected the interior walls from the fork trucks. Within minutes I found two ½" nuts.

I brought them back to the *Xerox Fuser Lab* and hung them directly in front of the vortex. The technician hooked up a recorder and a thermocouple to record the temperature.

The snow was flying, and the temperature was at minus forty degrees Fahrenheit. The threaded hole with the threads was totally iced up, along with the outer edges.

It was just after 10:00 am, and I called June, the secretary for the *Program High Volume Copier Manager*. I stated for her to take a 3"x5" card and put this message on it, "Today's date and time, Vortex set up in the *Xerox Fuser Lab* and currently running at minus forty degrees Fahrenheit. This will only be set up for ten minutes." I told her to give that message to Stanley. June stated, "He was in a staff meeting and he could not be disturbed."

I then stated, "Take the card in to him and he will make a decision."

Within minutes, he was in the *Xerox Fuser Lab*.

Immediately he was looking at the *vortex* and the snow flying around the heavy icing of the hardware I had hung in there.

He then stated, "He wanted to take my *vortex* apart and understand the theories and principles of applied engineering. He was missing my point.

I then mentioned, "When I shut this vortex down, there is going to be a lot of water all over the place. I was not sure that he was paying attention to me.

I then said to Stanley, "I get you down here, frost your n u t # and you still don't want to listen to me!" Yes, I said it. Ten seconds later he busted out laughing.

The blower-fan from the *9900 High Volume Duplicator* worked well and resolved the air flow and heat problem.

About three weeks later, Clark a manager that I had little contact with, said to me in the aisle, "What do you know about vortex engineering?" I instantly knew where this came from, I just showed my teeth, grinned and walked away with a huge smile.

Finding your funny side can make you appear more competent and confident, it will strengthen your relationship, unlock creativity, and make you more likeable. With professional work it is also thought that it is too risky to unleash your humor, therefore know your colleagues well.

"Being Good Natured is the Key to Effectiveness."

Donald A. Drexler

Marking Imaging Program
Reliability Manager ~ Xerox Corporation

Donald A. Drexler

Chapter XXIX - The Xerox Jaws Chart

(Titled after the Movie)

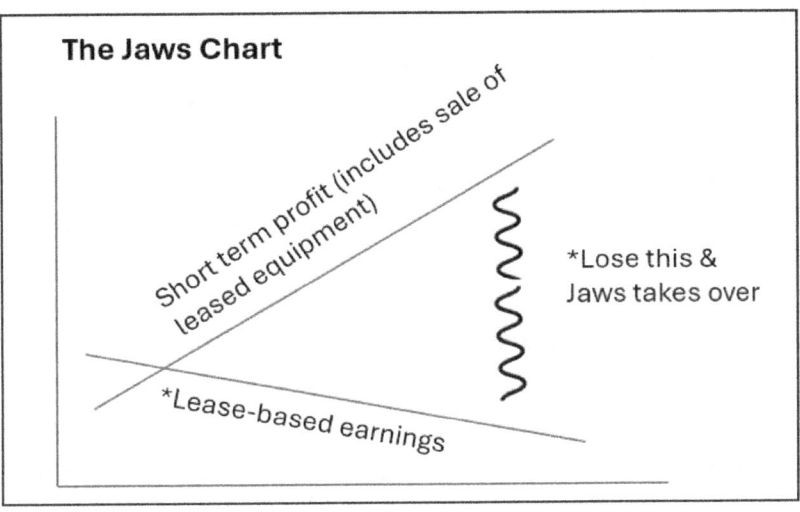

It did not take long, and this was known as the *Xerox Jaws Chart*, like the movie "Jaws." At *Xerox,* officers and executives would draw this to make clear what would happen if we did not keep up with technology. The line going up represents profits and benefits. The line going down represents the income or lease base, this from a financial standpoint, is what *Xerox Corporation* always referred to as its *"Annuity for the Future."*

That was drawn then, to show what will happen and, I don't need to say anything more, you guessed it, and it happened. There were some union workers that thought this was just a distraction to curb union demands. In the late seventies the company salvaged useful copiers, converting them for sale. The profit picture looked good then, but at the expense of leased or rental copiers. Jaws was chewing up earnings in the late seventies. *Xerox Rank* was looking at new products. The *Xerox 1075* and the *Xerox 1045* were scheduled, but slow to market. A lot was blamed on currencies and bad economics. The *Xerox 8200* was launched which looked good, but profits needed a boost, and the Japanese were a threat without question. The struggle went on and finally we began looking at what *Fuji Xerox* was doing, that was *Quality Control*. This became a *New Model for Xerox Corporation.*

Most of the models were dictated from the top down with no input from below. During the early 1980's the world had economic and currency struggles, that didn't help. *Rank Xerox* lost a billion and a half dollars in revenue. We had excellent strategies that were well thought out, but our plans didn't mesh. *Xerox* had difficulties getting products out the door. We needed to pay attention to our customers. We thought we had an answer, the *9400 Duplicator* was announced, and it worked well, but strategies needed to be addressed.

If I remember, *Xerox Corporation* then reported record net earnings of $598 million in 1981. Then the Jaws phenomenon or reality cut the profit or benefit to $424 million. A third-generation copier, the *10 Series* could then boost the company profits into late 1983. The *Webster New York Manufacturing Division* then found the Japanese were selling their copiers at our basic manufacturing cost. This was not good; you get the picture. Many times, I thought our duplicators were too big and complex, let alone the cost. We needed to rethink customer requirements. When I say complex, my percentage problem was 70% mechanical. I believe the more complex a machine is, the more problems you have. Another problem was, I did not like or appreciate the new demands of the *Amalgamated Clothing and Textile Workers Union,* and they did not realize their future when they thought of their demands over everything else.

Why I Wasn't Fired at Xerox

Today you can drive through the old *Xerox Manufacturing Complex* in *Webster, New York* (Buildings 208 and 200) the only vehicle you will see is a security car. At the time of this writing, the *Xerox Webster, New York Toner Plant* is still an active operation. I am surprised the manufacturing of copiers is very much alive with the stripping of the massive digital presses into new *iGens*. Along with this, the *Versa Link C8000W* is an *Office Color Printer,* and produces 45 copies per minute. Another product is the *Alta Link* copier along with many more. You can go online to find *Xerox copiers* that the Japanese, now have trouble competing with.

I also noticed that *Xerox Corporation* has expanded their partnership in Latin America with the *BS Group* in Peru and Ecuador.

~

To my knowledge, you will not find the Jaws Chart in the Xerox Nostalgia web-site.

Donald A. Drexler

Chapter XXX - Our President Archie McCardell (* real name) ~ Liked by 50% and disliked by the other half ~

Our *Chief Operating Officer* at the time was *Archie McCardell* who left *Ford Motor Company* in 1966. *McCardell* filled a lot of *Xerox* offices with *Ford Motor Company* personnel. His people were monolithic, functionalized, and bureaucratic. He had turf battles and insisted on rigid adherence to rules and forms. He created relationship problems with the *Amalgamated Clothing and Textile Workers Union* causing a strike. This was a low point when people like me were trying to create unity. I did not like his management style.

James Abegglen (* real name) an analyst told *Archie McCardell (*who was headstrong) that in *Japan* there would be a hell of a market with a smaller copier than the *914* with a good price tag. *McCardell*'s response to *Abegglen* was, "So what?" This was laughed off.

Abegglen also mentioned that "*Xerox* should give away the *914* copiers" and make its profit with supplies. That would counter the Japanese, leaving them little room to bring to market, a small copier. *McCardell* ignored the Japanese threat. In the early 1970 *Cannon* and *Konishiroku* copiers did not work very well. They did not have the technology. Note: *Konishiroku* was the predecessor of *Konica*. *Xerox* didn't react, and that is when *Xerox* started to lose benefits and earnings. *Archie McCardell* and the other guys from *Ford,* caught a lot of criticism, because they ignored what the Japanese were doing.

Archie McCardell was given the President's title… that was a mistake. As we were expanding in *Webster, New York,* the *Manufacturing Complex,* it was recommended (from the *Ford* folks) to install in building 200 a track system as *Ford* had, to move cars along their Production Line. This was done at great expense, then <u>never</u> <u>used</u>. You might say the complexity of a copier was overlooked or ignored.

After about six years *Archie McCardell* left in 1977 to become the head of *International Harvester,* where he incited a similar series of management failures, that included a ruinous five-month strike. In five years, he took *International Harvester* to the brink of bankruptcy. Six years later *International Harvester's* Board of Directors finally forced him out.

At that time *Xerox Headquarters* was in Rochester, New York, close to the *Manufacturing Plant* in *Webster, New York.* Then an old nemesis of his at *Xerox Corporation,* threw a ceremonial party to commemorate *Archie's* (lack of) management skills.

The party had to be broken up by the police.

I would have also liked to throw a party, but not as rowdy. The only thing that stopped me was the long hours I was putting in with the *Xerox High-Volume Copier / Duplicator* products.

~

Donald A. Drexler

Senior Engineer, High Volume Copier / Duplicator Xerox Corporation

Chapter XXXI - An Electronic Christmas Card

Sent to *Xerox* EL Segundo

A little background about the writer; at age eight I built a radio, it worked very well with and without headphones, it just seemed I was not interested in electronics. At age nine, I was repairing three and four speed transmissions on *English Raleigh* bicycles. About five years later, I was rebuilding transmissions (automatic and manual) in motor vehicles. It seemed I was not satisfied with either electrical or mechanical accomplishments and I wanted to be involved with the engineering aspects. I was motivated by my father, and if a proposed solution became complicated, that would capture my attention and I valued it, all the more.

My father constantly inspired and guided me with the above. Now getting into the electrical and mechanical engineering aspects with what he was teaching me, would be something different, especially, when it came to mathematics. In elementary school my math teacher hated me. She thought I was a *"Problem Child"* because, I worked the math problems the way my father taught me, and "not" by the way she wanted the mathematical problems solved. I was constantly getting zeros, but I had the correct answers. I could not win.

I took the *New York State Regents, Mathematics Exam* and had most of the answers in my head, before anything was put on paper. I thought I would have a good score. When the test results were announced, they started with the top score, to the bottom score (flunking - more than one). My score was <u>not</u> included. Then, she said, "We had to have three people look at *Don Drexler's* test," all three people agreed, "He did not push hard enough for a decimal point." She was out to get me, and of course she did. I looked at the test paper and you could see a slight indent in the paper, but no lead mark. (This was when you held the paper up to reflected light on the paper, you could see a slight indent.) I suspected a soap eraser was involved.

~ I made *National Honors.* ~

Now let's talk about the *Moving Electronic Christmas Card.* During *November of 1987* all I can remember of anything that would move electronically on a computer screen was the game called *"Pong."* What I can remember about this game was you had to control a ball as it moved back and forth. This game was simple. However, the electronic *Christmas Card* was a massive amount of programming. As you opened the card, it would show an evening sky, with a town below, and streetlights glowing. Soon appeared Santa's reindeer moving through the evening sky, while Santa was throwing gifts from the sleigh. The gifts would go down into the chimneys, (with smoke rising from them) and then windows in the homes would light up. The electronic card closed with the following words, "Merry Christmas and Happy New Year, from Donald A. Drexler, *Xerox Marking Imaging, Reliability Engineering Manager, Webster, New York."*

This *Christmas Card* was a monster of electronic data with seven drive engines and over nine thousand disk pages to make it work. At the time, I was using a double drive, double density "eight-inch" floppy. This type of floppy (or disk) is unheard of today. If you were to inquire about this type of floppy, I would think 80% plus, of computer users would not know of its existence today.

With something different, I wanted to demonstrate what could be done electronically to some of my managers. If I could inspire or influence my managers' thinking, it would be in line with the true leadership of *Joseph C. Wilson's* philosophy, our founder of *Xerox Corporation.*

This in a sense was a "Once in a Lifetime" opportunity. I just wanted to show there would be possibilities in the future. The card was sent.

With the electronic card, I made sure the instructions were clear and that was, "to move the electronic *"Christmas Card"* from the *Computer Main Frame* to each desktop, and make sure the seven drive engines were turned on, before opening it."

At the same time, I discovered in the *Xerox Phone Book* the name of a foster child, named Nancy, that lived next to me many years before. I decided to send the *"Christmas Card"* to her at *El Segundo, California*, after hours.

She received it on a Saturday after work and mailed a return letter back to me. She was delighted and surprised with the electronic technology involved. That *Christmas* became just a little extra special for her.

That Saturday evening, she decided to send my *"Christmas Card"* to some of her friends at *El Segundo*.

The following week on Tuesday I was informed by our *Program Vice President* that I had, "Shut Down" the *Xerox El Segundo Computer System* on Monday. This was from the *Xerox El Segundo Vice President,* and because of the computer "Shut Down" consequently, a chilling effect was sent in my direction. Let me say, I was deep in cold water, and I had to think of a way to redeem myself.

I called the *Xerox El Segundo Vice President* the next day (after the dust settled) and mentioned, I had very clear instructions, "to move the electronic *"Christmas Card,"* from the *Computer Main Frame* to each desktop, and make sure the seven drive engines were turned on, before opening it."

My instructions followed the *Xerox El Segundo Computer System Instruction Manual,* and if complied with, the system would not have crashed. I also mentioned "his" division wrote the *"Star Computer" Instruction Manual*, and those instructions were the same as mine.

The *Xerox El Segundo Vice President,* then said, "I have a problem at this end, I need to address," and wished me "a Very Merry Christmas and a Happy New Year." His words and his respect for me, I will never forget. I returned the salutation, and we were instant friends. It's always, when, and how you say it, Savoir-faire.

Today, 35 years later, I-phones can send digital versions of greeting cards and even include animation.

"You can always do Something Good, by Inspiring and Striving for a Better World."

Donald A. Drexler

Marking Imagining
Program Reliability Manager ~ Xerox Corporation

The Xerox Award
"It's a Miracle"
Award Picture from the Drexler Gallery

One of the many awards at Xerox Corporation.

In 1975 Brother Dominic launched, "It's a Miracle"
Campaign for the Xerox 9200 Duplicator.

Donald A. Drexler

APPENDIX I - The Xerox 914 / 720 Copier-

Some of the early History

The first *Xerox 914 Copier* was introduced to the public in 1959 and this was the very first floor model or office copier which made a copy every 26 seconds. Normal paper usage was with 8 ½" x 11" and it could produce copies up to 9" x 14." The *Xerox 914*-floor model or office copier was superior in quality with exceptional characteristics and could make about 100,000 copies per month. The *Xerox 914 Copier* tended to cause a fire now and then because of overheating and a drive system that contributed to the fires. I loved to refer to this as, *"Setting the world on fire."* *Haloid Xerox* gave or provided a *"Scorch Eliminator"* which was a fire extinguisher along with each copier. Customers didn't mind a fire once in a while; they just wanted (a new term) "Dry Copies." Dry copies would be the end of mimeograph, stencil printing or carbon copies. To make a copy all you had to do was place your original on the platen glass and press a button. Initially *Haloid Xerox* paid a lot of attention to function and to get the copier to the customer. One item overlooked was interchange ability and this became the top objective with replacement of parts/assemblies in the early stages of the *Xerox 914* copiers.

The *Xerox 720* was a slightly faster copier; I loved referring to this machine as a *"Souped-up Model."*

~

For more information about the Xerox 914 and 720 Copiers go to
https://xeroxnostalgia.com/2015/02/08/xerox-914/

Donald A. Drexler

APPENDIX II - The Xerox 813 Desktop

Copier-Some of the early History

The first *Xerox 813 Desktop Copier* was introduced to the public in October 1963. This machine was a desktop copier and could only make copies of originals, (one page at a time) not from books, or anything bound. To make a copy you had to enter the number of copies required. You would then feed the original into the gripper bar that held the original in position for the copies required. The *Xerox* logo appeared on the copy from the gripper bar, you knew it was a *Xerox* copy. This was a great way to advertise your product, but short lived. The original you fed into the copier returned to you in a slot in the front of the copier and the copies came out in a slot right beneath where the original returned to you. Weight of the *Xerox 813 Desktop Copier* was a massive 190 pounds that took two strong men to place it on a desk. You might say the weight of the copier was because of the many stainless-steel parts built into the copier. Fires you might say were eliminated. The last major production run of this copier was in 1971. *Chapter VII Unleashing a Radical Engineer* details some of the production problems. This was the last *Production Run* in the *Xerox Webster New York* complex, for the *Xerox 813 Desktop Copier.*

~

For more information about the Xerox 813 Desktop Copier go to
https://xeroxnostalgia.com/2015/02/08/xerox-813/

Donald A. Drexler

APPENDIX III - The Xerox 2400 Duplicator

Some of the early History

The first *Xerox 2400 Duplicator* was introduced to the public in October 1963. This was the very first duplicator. The "2400" denoted the number of copies per hour, 40 per minute or 2400 per hour. This duplicator could be furnished with a standard bin collator or sorter, and various solid color front doors were available. I often thought the sorter was of a primitive design but worked well. It was years later when we collated with offset copies eliminating a massive sorter assembly.

It should be noted I believe that the photograph of the *2400 Duplicator* in the *Xerox 2400 Nostalgia web-site* is not a *Xerox 2400 Duplicator*, but a *Xerox 3600 Duplicator*. The *Xerox 2400 Duplicator* had a curved platen glass with an elastic platen cover to protect your eyes from flash lamp exposure. The *Xerox 2400 Duplicator* did not have an *Automatic Document Feeder (ADF)* as shown. The photograph shown is a *Xerox 3600 Duplicator* with *ADF*. The *ADF* is the box on the work surface on the duplicator.

The initial design was intended to produce copies from roll paper. This roll was the equivalent of a case of paper, or 10,000 copies. This design never made it to market. A very fast and extremely sharp slitter (razor edge) would be required. Paper dust and a dull cutter would be a problem. Another problem was with the right mixture of air, paper dust and a static spark could cause fire. Another problem was how a young lady (or key operator) could lift a roll of paper (equivalent to 10,000 sheets) and assemble it into the *Xerox 2400 Duplicator* without causing harm/damage.

These problems would be resolved by using standard-sized paper. Various drive systems (that transport paper) in the *Xerox 2400 Duplicator* were improved, this was a major step with customer satisfaction.

Initially I thought that this duplicator would set the pace, well above competition. It sure did, but our design team was thinking years ahead with the advancement of technology. You might say it was about fixing and effectivity that was constantly thought of daily.

~

For more information about the Xerox 2400 Duplicator go to
XEROX 2400 NOSTALGIA
https://xeroxnostalgia.com/category/2400/

APPENDIX IV - The Xerox 5400 Copier

Duplicator Some of the early History

The first *Xerox 5400* was introduced to the public in July 1977. This copier/duplicator was an upgraded member of the 4000 family of copiers. It could produce 45 copies per minute. There were 2 paper trays that held 500 sheets each. The sorter was vertical with 20 bins. It utilized the same drive engine as the 4000 copiers. We developed a better (brush) process for cleaning the photoreceptor or drum. This was an improvement, but with problems. We needed to rethink the cleaning process, especially with electrostatic spark (static charge) that caused fires with the right mixture of toner and air, this was a top priority. One of my responsibilities was with the optics assembly. I had major problems with the optics bearings. You may refer the *Chapter XVII, A Bearing That Stopped Everything*.

~

For more information about the Xerox 5400 Copier Duplicator go to
https://xeroxnostalgia.com/category/5400/

Donald A. Drexler

APPENDIX V - The *Xerox 5090 Copier*

Duplicator - Some of the early History

The first *Xerox 5090 Copier Duplicator* was introduced to the public in October 1979. The *Xerox 5090* (nick named the *Power House*) was a medium volume copier/duplicator and was controlled by seven computers. This statement I will accept, however it was seven microprocessors.

I managed the *Installation and Inspection* verification of the *Master Computer*, that checked over 9000 circuits in the seven computers or microprocessors that talked to each other. Initial testing was a total failure with failures that would not repeat themselves. All I had was random numbers, without a fix to the cause. The answers to the failures are well documented in Chapter XIX. My assignment was to make sure it worked flawlessly. I don't like to admit this, but I discovered the cause by accident, after I had worked two double shifts and was extremely tired. Perseverance paid off.

With this copier/duplicator, you could scan ahead with multiple jobs, send faxes at the same time while printing. When a job is running, you could program many additional jobs, unload jobs, load new jobs, maximizing uptime. You could create various shades of gray (very light to very dark) for graphs or charts and have smooth transitions with photographs. The *Xerox 5090* had automatic reduction and enlargement features. At one point I thought that this copier / duplicator had little room for technical advancement. I was wrong, never underestimate a brilliant *Xerox Design Department*.

The *Xerox 5090 Copier/Duplicator* was certainly the premier of all duplicating systems. The copy rate was 135 copies per minute. The Copier/Duplicator utilized a full color Touch Control Screen that would help you make use of its many features. The machine had 3 paper trays, a duplex tray, and a 4,300-sheet paper supply. The machine offered permanent thermal adhesive binding of books from 15 pages to 125 pages and had an *Automatic Document Feeder (ADF)*. This machine had top level of diagnostic testing and automatic adjustment for key functions. In other words, a technician would not have to show up when there is paper dust on a light sensor, it automatically adjusted itself, by increasing the voltage.

~

For more information about the Xerox 5090 Copier Duplicator go to
https://xeroxnostalgia.com/category/5090/

APPENDIX VI - The Xerox DocuTech 135

Production Publisher

The first *Xerox DocuTech 135 Production Publisher* was introduced to the public in October 1990. The *Xerox DocuTech* (Digital Press) was the worlds, first fully automatic, plain paper photocopier, with high resolution scanning, lazer imaging that delivered offset like quality. This allowed for lower cost and unprecedented turnaround time.

The *DocuTech* made it possible to receive electronic images of documents from remote computers, store them and allow them to be edited and shared over computer networks, and then generate documents of print-shop quality at high speed. Once there was no viable way for a printer to print directly from a computer to a high-speed production printer.

The printing process was forever revised by the *DocuTech 135 Production Publisher.*

My assignment was with *Marking Imagining* for *Managing Reliability* with the *Xerox DocuTech 135 Program.* The *Xerox Program Design Team* that I worked with were brilliant and many revolutionary patents were the result of their thinking. Today the *Xerox DocuTech 135* is still the finest digital press on the market.

~

For more information about the *Xerox DocuTech 135* go to

https://digitalprinting.blogs.xerox.com/2015/10/02/celebrating-25-year-anniversary-xerox-docutech/

Donald A. Drexler

Why I Wasn't Fired at Xerox

Starry Night Publishing

Everyone has a story...

Don't spend your life trying to get published! Don't tolerate rejection! Don't do all the work and allow the publishing companies to reap the rewards!

Millions of independent authors like you are making money, publishing their stories now. Our technological know-how will take the headaches out of getting published. Let Starry Night Publishing take care of the hard parts, so you can focus on writing. You simply send us your Word Document, and we do the rest. It really is that simple!

The big companies want to publish only "celebrity authors," not the average book-writer. It is almost impossible for first-time authors to get published today. This has led many authors to go the self-publishing route. Until recently, this was considered "vanity-publishing." You spent large sums of your money to get twenty copies of your book, to give to relatives at Christmas just so you could see your name on the cover. However, the self-publishing industry allows authors to get published in a timely fashion, retain the rights to your work, keeping up to ninety percent of your royalties instead of the traditional five percent.

We have opened the gates, allowing you inside the world of publishing. While others charge you as much as fifteen-thousand dollars for a publishing package, we charge less than five-hundred dollars to cover copyright, ISBN, and distribution costs. Do you really want to spend all your time formatting, converting, designing a cover, and then promoting your book because no one else will?

Our editors are professionals, able to create a top-notch book that you will be proud of. Becoming a published author is supposed to be fun, not a hassle.

At Starry Night Publishing, you submit your work, we create a professional-looking cover, a table of contents, compile your text and images into the appropriate format, convert your files for eReaders, take care of copyright information, assign an ISBN, allow you to keep one-hundred-percent of your rights, distribute your story worldwide on Amazon, Barnes and Noble and many other retailers, and write you a check for your royalties. There are no other hidden fees involved! You do not pay extra for a cover or to keep your book in print. We promise! Everything is included! You even get a free copy of your book and unlimited half-price copies.

In twelve short years, we have published more than six thousand books, compared to the major publishing houses, which only add an average of six new titles per year. We will publish your fiction or non-fiction books about anything and look forward to reading your stories and sharing them with the world.

We do all subject matter, fiction, or nonfiction, scholarly works, cookbooks, self-help, etc. Our company might not be huge in size, but we currently have more than 6,500 clients, maintain an A+ rating with the Better Business Bureau, of which we are an accredited member, and have won the "Best of Rochester" Business Award four years in a row, making us a member of the Rochester Business Hall of Fame.

We sincerely hope that you will join the growing Starry Night Publishing family, become a published author, and gain the world-wide exposure that you deserve. You deserve to succeed. Success comes to those who make opportunities happen, not those who wait for opportunities to happen. You just have to try. Thanks for joining us on our journey.

www.starrynightpublishing.com

www.facebook.com/starrynightpublishing/

Made in the USA
Middletown, DE
09 December 2025

22246064R00119